FACTS AT YOUR
FINGERTIPS

THE WORLD OF ENDANGERED ANIMALS

AUSTRALIA AND SOUTHEAST ASIA

BROWN
BEAR
BOOKS

Published by Brown Bear Books Limited

4877 N. Circulo Bujia
Tucson, AZ 85718
USA

and

First Floor
9-17 St. Albans Place
London N1 ONX
UK

ISBN-13 978-1-78121-078-9

In this book you will see the following key at top left of each entry. The key shows the level of threat faced by each animal, as judged by the International Union for the Conservation of Nature (IUCN).

EX	Extinct
EW	Extinct in the Wild
CR	Critically Endangered
EN	Endangered
VU	Vulnerable
NT	Near Threatened
LC	Least Concern
O	Other (this includes Data Deficient [DD] and Not Evaluated [NE])

For a few animals that have not been evaluated since 2001, the old status of Lower Risk still applies and this is shown by the letters **LR** on the key.

For more information on Categories of Threat, see pp. 54–57.

Editorial Director: Lindsey Lowe
Editor: Tim Harris
Design Manager: Keith Davis
Designer: Lynne Lennon
Children's Publisher: Anne O'Daly
Production Director: Alastair Gourlay

Printed in the United States of America

062014
AG/5534

Picture Credits

Cover Images
Front: *Victoria crowned pigeon,* Dariush M./Shutterstock
Back: *Leadbeater's possum,* Jason Edwards/Alamy

Alamy: John Cancalosi 54–55; **FLPA:** Hiroya Minakuchi/Minden Pictures 11, Colin Monteath/Minden Pictures, Martin White 41; **Getty Images:** Patricio Robles 37, Lonely Planet 49; **Photoshot:** Gerald Cubitt 1, 47, ANT Photolibrary/NHPA 13, 15, 17, Ken Griffiths 45; **Shutterstock:** Ekaterina Kamenetsky 4, Edward Haylan 4–5, Piotr Gatlik 7, Andrea Izzotti 9, Julian W 19, Mountain Pix 25, Mircea Bezergneanu 33, Api Guide 35, Cameramannz 38–39, John Austin 43, Tony Bowler 57, GTS Production 59.

Artwork © Brown Bear Books Ltd

Brown Bear Books has made every attempt to contact the copyright holder. If anyone has any information please contact smortimer@windmillbooks.co.uk

CONTENTS

Habitats, Threats, and Conservation

Southeast Asia and the many islands of Indonesia, along with the huge islands of Borneo and New Guinea, have one of the most diverse ranges of mammals, birds, reptiles, and amphibians anywhere on Earth. The equator runs just north of New Guinea and bisects Borneo, peninsular Malaysia, and Sumatra. This region, and the northernmost part of Australia, has a humid tropical climate. It was once much more extensively forested than now; the forest has been much reduced as a result of human activities: logging for lumber; burning for agriculture; and clearance for cities and roads. Bali, for example, home of the Critically Endangered Bali starling, has had most of its forest cleared. In 2012 Indonesia had the highest rate of deforestation in the world.

Mountain ranges

Many of the tropical islands have chains of high mountains—for example, the Crocker Range on Borneo and the Pegunungan Maoke on New Guinea. These are important for biodiversity, especially that of birds, with some species living only at mid- or high altitudes. In 2011 the crow honeyeater, a bird thought to have been extinct for decades, was rediscovered on forested Mount Panié on the island of New

Caledonia. There are also alpine grasslands surrounding New Guinea's highest peaks, supporting a variety of rare mammals and birds: MacGregor's bird of paradise and Papuan thornbill are two such examples. Mountain forests are equally important in mainland Southeast Asia, with the Bilauktang Range of Thailand, the Annam Cordillera of Laos and Vietnam, and the Cameron Highlands in Malaysia. These ranges are hard to access, and even harder to farm, so deforestation has been slower than in the lowlands. These highlands have provided the last sanctuaries for some animals. Some lowland areas are seasonally flooded, providing habitats for many fish, aquatic birds, and reptiles. Coastal mangroves are another important habitat in Southeast Asia and north Australia.

There are many protected areas, although some have suffered from illegal logging and poaching in the past. Way Kambas National Park, in Sumatra, has populations of Critically Endangered Sumatran tigers, elephants, and rhinoceroses, and Endangered White-winged Ducks. West Bali National Park was established to offer protection to the Bali starling. And Daintree Rainforest reserve in Queensland is home to one-third of Australia's frog, marsupial, and reptiles species and two-thirds of its bats and butterflies.

Suburbs of cities *such as Sydney and Brisbane have spread far into rural areas, destroying much animal-rich habitat.*

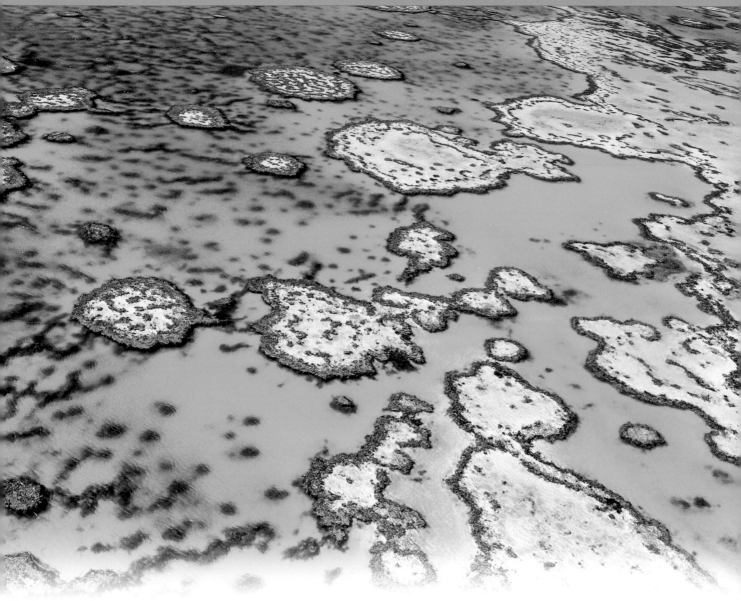

Australia

In addition to its tropical forests Australia has extensive temperate forests in the states of Victoria and New South Wales. These support a healthy diversity of animals, including some species with very limited ranges. For example, Leadbeater's possum (Endangered) is restricted to wet eucalypt forests in the Central Highlands of Victoria; and the swift parrot (Endangered) migrates to this region from Tasmania each winter. Damaging wildfires, harmful agricultural management, alluvial gold mining, and alien and feral rabbits, foxes,

The Great Barrier Reef, *off the coast of Queensland, Australia, is that country's largest protected area.*

and cats are all threats to the animals of these forests, as is sprawling urban development. Much of the land has already been turned into arable farmland or pasture, and the introduced rabbits have overgrazed vegetation, making it tougher for the native grazing animals to find food. Protected areas include national parks at Grampians and Wilson's Promontory in Victoria and Wadbilliga, Deua, and Morton in New South Wales.

The Wallace Line

Australia and the islands of New Guinea, Sulawesi, Halmahera, and Flores are separated from the islands of Borneo, Bali, Java, Sumatra, and the mainland of Southeast Asia by an invisible line, the Wallace Line. This is named for the British naturalist Alfred Russel Wallace, who recognized that the mix of animals one side of it were very different from those on the other side. This is especially true for mammals and birds. For example, the native mammals of Australia and New Guinea are marsupials; those to the northwest of the line are not. During ice ages, when ice sheets expanded at high latitudes, the sea level fell and the islands to the northwest of the Wallace Line became joined in one landmass, as did those to the southeast. Even then, however, a trench of deep ocean still separated the two areas of land, as it had for more than 50 million years. That separation had allowed species to evolve separately—and differently—on either side.

Above the tree line in the Great Dividing Range of Victoria and New South Wales is high-altitude alpine grassland. Here, conditions are mild for much of the year but there is snow cover in winter. The Critically Endangered marsupial Mountain Pygmy-possum lives near Mount Bogong and Mount Higginbotham.

Semiarid grassland and desert stretch across Australia's vast interior. Much of the natural grassland has been turned over to arable farming or the grazing of animals. Some native animals have suffered as a result of these changes—for example, the plains-wanderer, a ground-living bird now classified as Endangered. Areas of suitable habitat (low plants with plentiful bare patches) are just a small fraction of what they once were. In good years plains-wanderer numbers may reach 7,000, but in years of harsh drought they may fall to only 2,000. Another Endangered bird of this environment is the night parrot, whose nocturnal lifestyle makes it very difficult to estimate its population.

The Australian interior (or 'Outback') can experience scorching daytime temperatures and long periods without rain—although when it falls, the rain may be torrential. Despite these challenging conditions this environment supports large numbers of animals. Many remain in underground burrows during the day, only becoming active at night. This is the domain of many reptile species, including bearded dragons, perenties, and thorny devils, which have grooves in their body scales to channel dew to their mouth.

The Great Barrier Reef lies off the northeast coast of Australia and is the largest coral reef on Earth, stretching 1,600 miles (2,575 km). The reef's biodiversity is extraordinary, including more than 1,500 species of fish, 17 species of sea snake, 30 different kinds of dolphin and whale, and a healthy population of dugongs. It is protected by law but, as with all reefs, is likely to suffer as global ocean temperatures rise as a result of climate change.

New Zealand

The two main islands of New Zealand (North Island and South Island) have big areas of temperate forest and high-altitude meadows on mountains such as the Kaikoura Ranges. New Zealand's only native mammals are three species of bat, but one of the biggest threats to the country's fauna has come from introduced mammals: rats, cats, and dogs, especially since many native birds are flightless. This threat explains why so many native animals now live only on rocky offshore islands. These natives include the tuatara, a reptile in a family of its own, and the Critically Endangered kakapo, a nocturnal flightless parrot that is adept at climbing trees. Several hundred miles southeast of New Zealand, the small Chatham Islands are home to many seabirds, including Chatham Islands taiko and Chatham petrel, which breed nowhere else.

A termite nest in Kakadu National Park, Australia. Several endangered mammals, birds, and reptiles live in this preserve.

Dugong

Dugong dugon

The vegetarian dugong has been hunted to the brink of extinction throughout most of its range. The future of the species may now rest almost exclusively with the fate of one population living off the coast of Australia.

Sightings of dugongs and their kind are often said to have given rise to stories of mermaids. The large, blubbery animals, with their huge bristle-studded lips and tough, gray hide, may be far removed from the traditional image of the fabled sea maidens, but dugongs are nevertheless graceful, gentle, and curious animals. In areas where they are not persecuted they readily approach divers and small boats, apparently attracted by unusual sounds. Dugongs have excellent hearing and good eyesight.

The dugong's alternative name of "sea cow" is fitting, since the animal's behavior reflects that of the land cow. Like its land-dwelling namesake, it lives mostly in herds and it feeds on underwater pastures of sea grass. It has intelligence similar to a cow or deer, and its flesh is reputed to taste much like veal.

The dugong is the only living species in its family. Its closest relative, Steller's sea cow, was hunted to extinction over a period of just 27 years during the 18th century.

Hunting and Natural Hazards

At one time dugongs were common around the edges of the Indian and southwestern Pacific Oceans. However, dugongs make good eating and have other uses. They have been hunted for meat, their oil, and their thick hides, which produce good leather. Dugongs are mammals, so they have to breathe air. Consequently, when they come up from a dive to breathe at the surface, they are easy to catch and kill in nets. The dugong has now been brought to the brink of extinction across its range.

Dugongs also face a number of natural hazards. In the past, when the animals were common, the population could withstand losses from predation by sharks, killer whales, and estuarine crocodiles. It could even recover from local catastrophes, such as flooded rivers that dumped thousands of tons of silt over their sea grass pastures, causing mass starvation. Today, with so many dugong populations at the very limit of viability, such pressures could mean extinction for the remaining groups.

The plight of the African and Asian populations is cause for extreme concern. In 1998 it was reported that the last remaining viable population of East African dugongs had probably declined to just 21 individuals—barely a sustainable number. Around the coasts of Madagascar, India, Sri Lanka, and Southeast Asia the situation is equally critical. The dugong is protected by law throughout its range, but in many areas the law is difficult to enforce. Illegal killing undoubtedly still occurs, sometimes by accident, sometimes deliberately in order to obtain food, hides, and body parts for use in traditional medicines and treatments; substances derived from the dugong are used as aphrodisiacs.

Last Stronghold

Dugongs once lived around the Australian coast in great herds numbering many thousands of individuals. Although such herds are almost certainly a thing of the past, groups of several hundred dugongs are still reported off the coast of western Australia. However, it is the seas between Australia's northern coast and

DATA PANEL

Dugong (sea cow)

Dugong dugon

Family: Dugongidae

World population: Probably fewer than 150,000

Distribution: Indian and southwestern Pacific Oceans

Habitat: Shallow seas of tropical coasts

Size: Length head to tail: 8–9 ft (2.4–2.7 m), occasionally up to 13 ft (4 m) Weight: 300–800 lb (230–360 kg), occasionally up to 2,000 lb (900 kg)

Form: Large, superficially seal-like mammal with gray, almost hairless hide, jointed front flippers, and broad, flat tail. Small eyes and large upper lip with tough, bristly pads

Diet: Mostly sea grasses; occasionally green and brown seaweed

Breeding: Single young (rarely twins) born every 3–7 years at any time of year, after gestation of 13–14 months. Young first graze at 3 months; fully weaned at 18 months; mature at 9–10 years. Life span up to 73 years

Related endangered species: Steller's sea cow *(Hydrodamalis gigas)* EX. No close living relatives but 3 species of manatee listed as Vulnerable: Amazon manatee *(Trichechus inunguis)*, Florida manatee *(T. manatus)*, and African manatee *(T. senegalensis)*

Status: IUCN VU

the island of New Guinea that represent the closest thing the dugong has to a stronghold. Here a limited amount of hunting by native Australians and Torres Strait Islanders is still permitted. About 1,200 dugongs are killed in the region each year, mostly by nets or harpoons. Such hunting is strictly monitored because there are fears that even limited kills might be too much. It remains to be seen if hunting will result in the same fate for the dugong as it did for Steller's sea cow—extinction.

The dugong *uses its tail for swimming and its flippers for steering and "walking" along the seabed while it feeds. The tail has a distinctive concave trailing edge, which helps distinguish the dugong from the similar manatees.*

Goodfellow's Tree-kangaroo

Dendrolagus goodfellowi

One of the few kangaroos living outside Australia, Goodfellow's tree-kangaroo of Papua New Guinea is typical of several species that are threatened by hunting and habitat loss as logging and mining operations steadily encroach on their forest home.

Many people are surprised to learn that there are any kangaroos living as native species outside Australia. Goodfellow's tree-kangaroo is one of several that are found across the Torres Straits in Papua New Guinea. Like most other marsupials, Goodfellow's tree-kangaroo is largely nocturnal. It emerges from dense clusters of silkwood trees at dusk and gets around by means of a peculiar, rocking, hopping gait using both front and back legs. The tree-kangaroo does not use its tail as an extra limb to aid balance, so it is unable to take long series of bounding hops like its more familiar cousins. Relative awkwardness on the ground is the price the animal pays for surprising agility in the trees. By spending a good deal of their time off the ground, tree-kangaroos are relatively safe from predators and able to reach abundant food sources that are inaccessible to their earth-bound relatives.

The tree-kangaroos' unusual lifestyle made them very successful in the past, when their forest home extended from the highlands of eastern and central Papua New Guinea—where they are now found—down to sea level. The main factor controlling the population was the weather, which is extemely variable in this part of the tropics. The tree-kangaroos coped by having a variable reproductive rate. The females do not tend to breed when conditions are poor. However, since they are not tied to a particular breeding season, they are able to raise one baby every 10 or 11 months in a run of good years. Although unusual, Goodfellow's tree-kangaroo is, nevertheless, a fairly successful mammal species. As recently as the 1960s, before guns became widespread in Papua New Guinea, it was hunted using dogs and spears or arrows. Such traditional hunting took its toll, but had little effect on the total population. The rarity of tree-kangaroos today is a result of more recent developments.

Changing Landscape

The landscape of Papua New Guinea has changed dramatically in recent decades. Much of the lowland rain forest has already been cleared, and logging activities are now encroaching on the highlands, too. Papua New

DATA PANEL

Goodfellow's tree-kangaroo (ornate tree-kangaroo)

Dendrolagus goodfellowi

Family: Macropodidae

World population: Unknown, perhaps only a few hundred

Distribution: Eastern and central Papua New Guinea

Habitat: Lowland and montane (mountainous) rain forest up to about 10,000 ft (3,000 m)

Size: Length head/body: 21–30 in (55–77 cm); tail: 27.5–35 in (70–85 cm); females up to 20% bigger than males. Weight: 14–18 lb (6.5–8 kg)

Form: Small, slender kangaroo with shorter back legs and longer front legs than terrestrial species; fur short and reddish brown, fading to creamy-yellow on underside and feet; coat marked with 2 pale dorsal stripes and pale rings on tail

Diet: Leaves and fruit

Breeding: Single young born at any time of year after 3–5 week gestation; incubated in pouch for 10–12 months. Lives up to 14 years in captivity

Related endangered species: Other species of tree-kangaroo, including Doria's tree-kangaroo (*Dendrolagus dorianus*) VU; Scott's tree-kangaroo (*D. scottae*) CR; Bennett's tree-kangaroo (*D. Bennettianus*) NT

Status: IUCN EN

Guinea is also rich in mineral reserves, and huge mining and oil-extraction operations have added to the devastation. The settlements that spring up around the mining and logging industries mean that more land has to be cleared to grow crops to feed the people. Tree-kangaroos have always been prized for their meat, and with new roads and settlements appearing throughout the forest, more colonies are vulnerable to hunting than ever before. In some places tree-kangaroos have taken to eating cereal crops planted alongside their forest habitat, giving hunters an excuse to kill yet more of an increasingly endangered species. Goodfellow's tree-kangaroo has been wiped out of the areas surrounding even very small settlements in a short space of time. With logging and mining constantly eating away at the edge of the forest, the species' range is shrinking fast.

Goodfellow's tree-kangaroo *does not look or act much like the kangaroos and wallabies of Australia. It has traded the convenience of a hopping lifestyle for the security and plentiful food resources available in the trees.*

Tree-kangaroos do have some refuges in national parks and appear to be doing well in areas where they and their habitat are properly protected. The simple answer to the tree-kangaroo's problems would be to designate large areas of forest as protected land. However, much of the real power in Papua New Guinea lies not with the government but with the multinational corporations exploiting the country's mineral and timber resources. For such organizations conservation of a little-known marsupial is not a priority.

Leadbeater's Possum

Gymnobelideus leadbeateri

A long-lost animal whose particular habitat and lifestyle requirements have already given it one brush with extinction, Leadbeater's possum is now threatened again and in need of radical conservation measures to keep it from disappearing forever.

Leadbeater's possum was first described in 1867. It was extremely rare, and because of its nocturnal habits and largely inaccessible habitat only four more specimens were caught before 1921, when it was declared extinct. Most of its biology was still a mystery, as was its lifestyle.

Leadbeater's possums were so scarce in the 19th century for two main reasons. First, they have quite specific habitat requirements, and suitable homes were few and far between. These nimble marsupials live only in well-developed forests containing a tall species of eucalyptus known as mountain ash. They are completely dependent on an adequate supply of old, hollow trees in which to nest, and they need plenty of nearby wattle acacia scrub in which to feed. This combination was only available in a few limited areas of Victoria in southern Australia.

The second factor that limited their numbers was competition from other better-adapted possums, particularly the sugar glider. Changes in climate and vegetation types over the last two million years have shifted conditions in favor of the sugar gliders, which can "fly" between widely separated trees. The nongliding Leadbeater's possum can only jump comparatively short distances. The overall picture in the late 19th century was of a species whose time was up, and for once the decline appeared to have nothing to do with humans.

Rising from the Ashes

In 1939, 30 years after the last Leadbeater's possum was recorded, a devastating wildfire tore through the central highlands, destroying about 70 percent of the state of Victoria's forests. The fire was catastrophic, but while large areas of burned-out habitat were cleared, the rest began a steady regeneration.

DATA PANEL

Leadbeater's possum

Gymnobelideus leadbeateri

Family: Petauridae

World population: About 1,000, including 50 at Yellingbo, Victoria

Distribution: Central highlands of Victoria, Australia

Habitat: Australian mountain ash forest with dense undergrowth of wattle acacia

Size: Length head/body: up to 6 in (15 cm); tail: 6 in (15 cm). Weight: 2.5–6 oz (70–170 g)

Form: Guinea-pig-sized marsupial with long, furry tail, covered in thick, velvety-gray fur with dark stripe down back; eyes very large and black; female's pouch opens at front

Diet: Mostly insects; also sap, gum, and honeydew

Breeding: One or 2 young born at any time of year except midsummer; weaned at 3 months; mature at 2 years. Life span unknown, but probably about 5 years

Related endangered species: Mahogany glider *(Petaurus gracilis)* EN; Tate's triok *(Dactilopsila tatei)* EN

Status: IUCN EN

Dense scrub sprang up from the ashes, and new trees began to grow around the blackened trunks. After 20 years or so, and without anyone realizing it, huge tracts of habitat ideal for Leadbeater's possum were re-created. The standing dead wood left by the 1939 fire provided an abundance of nesting sites, while the fresh new growth yielded plenty of the gummy sap and hidden insects on which the possums could feed. From some secret refuge the species recovered, taking full advantage of this unexpected second chance. In 1961 a Leadbeater's possum—only the sixth specimen ever recorded—was spotted by delighted members of a local wildlife group.

By the mid-1980s there were an estimated 5,000 Leadbeater's possums living in Victoria, and extensive studies had revealed all kinds of fascinating facts about their biology. For example, unlike most mammals, it is the female that stakes out the breeding territory, aided by a faithful male and several of her sons.

Short-lived Success?

This was new and exciting information, but at the same time, other studies on the possums' new habitat suggested that their recovery would be short-lived. The old dead trees in which the possums live are collapsing at a rapid rate; and because the rest of the trees in the forest are still young, it will probably be over 100 years before the dead wood is replaced. In many areas the new forest has already begun to be logged. The population of Leadbeater's possum fell during the early years of the 21st century. Bush fires in 2009 destroyed 45 percent of suitable habitat, and numbers fell to about 1,000.

New forest-management plans are now being put in place to conserve the species in nature reserves, and the Australian government is under pressure to adopt possum-friendly logging practices in the state-owned forests where these intriguing mammals live.

Leadbeater's possum *is considered a relatively primitive species. It lacks many of the specializations shown by other possums, such as an elongated finger for extracting insects from under bark or a web of skin between its front and hind limbs that can be used for gliding.*

Long-footed Potoroo

Potorous longipes

One of the world's most recently described mammals, the long-footed potoroo is among Australia's rarest animals. Living in the dense undergrowth of wet forests, these tiny kangaroos try to avoid predators such as domestic dogs. Now inroads are being made into even their most remote refuges.

The long-footed potoroo is the rarest of the three surviving species of potoroo, or rat kangaroo, as they are sometimes known. Potoroos are marsupials and have pouches, but they are not as large as kangaroos: All are about the size of a rabbit, or even smaller. The young live in their mother's pouch for four or five months, then stay nearby until independent.

The long-footed potoroo was recognized as a distinct species as recently as 1978 and was only fully described in 1980. Such a fact may seem surprising, given that the only known colonies live in the relatively well-populated Australian states of New South Wales and Victoria. However, potoroos are extremely shy animals and live in dense vegetation in remote areas, where they are rarely disturbed by people. They forage at night, eating mainly fungi and plant material.

Dogs, foxes, and cats had not been introduced to Australia in the millions of years when the potoroos were evolving their quiet, fungus-eating way of life. Since Europeans began settling the continent, however, the domestic animals they took with them have posed a threat. Like many native Australian mammals, the potoroo is virtually defenseless against such effective predators. For a while the potoroo managed to evade extinction by retreating to the most inaccessible habitat it could find. Now, however, even the remotest hideaways are being exposed.

Nowhere to Hide

The habitats on which the potoroos rely are being spoiled as timber companies venture deeper into the forests to gain access to valuable hardwood trees. The roads built to allow the trees to be taken away carve up areas of pristine habitat and expose the insides of even very dense forests to disturbance.

The plight of the potoroo is just one of the reasons why the Australian timber industry is highly controversial. Only about 13 percent of the forest known to be home to long-footed potoroos is currently protected. The rest is all state-owned and as such can still be logged. Timber cutting in Australia is much more closely monitored than in many other countries, and there is less wholesale

DATA PANEL

Long-footed potoroo

Potorous longipes

Family: Potoroidae

World population: Probably only a few hundred

Distribution: Parts of southeastern Australia

Habitat: Wet forests at altitudes of 470–2,620 ft (150–800 m) with an annual rainfall of 43–47 in (110–120 cm)

Size: Length head/body: 15–17 in (38–41.5 cm); tail: about 12.5 in (32 cm); males 20% bigger than females. Weight: 3.5–4.8 lb (1.6–2.2 kg)

Form: Rabbit-sized kangaroo with thick, gray-brown fur and elongated back feet and toes

Diet: Mostly fungi; some invertebrates and plant material

Breeding: Single young born after estimated 38-day gestation; born at any time of year, though few arrive in the fall. Two or 3 births per female per year. Young spend up to 5 months in the pouch; mature at 2 years. Longevity unknown

Related endangered species: Gilbert's potoroo (*Potorous gilbertii*) CR; northern bettong (*Bettongia tropica*) EN

Status: IUCN EN

destruction of the sort that still occurs in South America and Southeast Asia. However, once a road has been built for the transportation of timber, the interior of the forest is no longer a refuge against intruding predators.

The Fight against Extinction

Today there are three known populations of long-footed potoroo in southeastern Australia. One was discovered as recently as 1995, so there is hope that there may still be other undiscovered populations hiding away elsewhere.

A number of conservation management plans are being investigated with the aim of preserving the habitats of the long-footed potoroo and its cousin, the long-nosed potoroo. Important measures include setting up protected areas from which predators are excluded and educating the public so that any sightings of the long-footed potoroo can be reported and used to get a clearer picture of the species' distribution and numbers. As a precaution against total extinction, a small colony of long-footed potoroos is being kept in captivity at a wildlife sanctuary in Victoria.

The long-footed potoroo *hops around on its back legs and uses the front ones for digging up underground fungi to eat.*

EX
EW
CR
EN
VU
NT
LC
O

Mountain Pygmy-possum

Burramys parvus

Life in the snow-covered Victorian Alps is hard for the rare mountain pygmy-possum. The tourist industry is increasing the pressure, but conservation authorities are working to provide solutions.

When the mountain pygmy-possum was first discovered in 1864, zoologists were mistaken in two respects. Since the species was described from a few 15,000-year-old fossils found in a cave in New South Wales, it was thought to be already extinct. In addition, from the limited evidence available the new animal was classed as a kind of miniature kangaroo. In the 1950s a reexamination of the fossils concluded that the species was in fact a kind of possum. It appeared that the mountain pygmy-possum had once been widespread throughout southeastern Australia, but as the climate warmed up, the habitat of snow-covered boulder slopes and alpine heaths where the possums lived became scarce. Zoologists had no inkling that living specimens might still be scuttling around in the wild until 1966, when a real live mountain pygmy-possum turned up in a ski lodge at a resort on Mount Hotham in Victoria, southern Australia.

Hidden Creatures

As well as being extremely rare, the mountain pygmy-possum is, by nature, an inconspicuous mammal. It is small, nocturnal, and spends six months of the year hibernating in a boulder crevice under a thick layer of snow. It has a total range of no more than 4 square miles (10 sq. km). Even this small range is broken up into several parts, each area being separated by tracts of unsuitable habitat.

The needs of the mountain pygmy-possum are quite specific. It lives at high altitudes in order to take advantage of the arrival in spring of millions of bogong moths, which migrate to the Victorian Alps to breed. The moths are large and nutritious, and the possums time their own breeding to coincide with the glut of food. Later in the summer, as the moths disappear, the possums turn their attention to the berries and seeds of plants that only grow in their mountain heath habitat. Late summer and early fall see the possums feeding frantically. They need to double their body weight if they are to survive the winter. As an extra insurance policy, the possums are known to cache certain types of food, presumably so they can find it during their brief periods of winter activity, or if spring arrives late.

DATA PANEL

Mountain pygmy-possum

Burramys parvus

Family: Burramyidae

World population: 2,250 in 2008

Distribution: Southeastern New South Wales and northern Victoria, Australia

Habitat: Dense, subalpine boulder slopes at altitudes of 4,600–7,200 ft (1,400–2,200 m); among heath vegetation and snow-gum shrubs

Size: Length head/body: 4–5 in (10–13 cm); tail: 5–6 in (13–15 cm). Weight: 1–2 oz (30–60 g)

Form: Tiny, mouselike possum with distinct pouch and long, mostly hairless prehensile tail; eyes large and black; ears large and rounded; fur grayish brown above and whitish on underside

Diet: Seeds, fruit, worms, insects, and other invertebrates

Breeding: Up to 8 young born November–December after gestation of 13–16 days; maximum of 4 incubated in pouch; young leave pouch at 3 weeks, weaned at 8–9 weeks. Females may live up to 12 years, males 4 years

Related endangered species: Long-tailed pygmy possum (*Cercartetus macrurus*) LC

Status: IUCN CR

A Fragile Existence

Despite all their preparation, many possums starve in winter; the death rate in males is four or five times as high as in females, simply because females occupy the best habitat. When they grow up, young males are driven out of their mother's home range and forced to live nomadic lives, eking out a living in marginal habitats. In spring they migrate back into female territories to mate.

Almost without exception, the areas in which the mountain pygmy-possum lives are prime sites for winter sporting activities, and efforts to conserve the species have required a good deal of negotiation and cooperation with the ski-tourism industry. Ski runs and roads break up areas of mountain pygmy-possum habitat and can present an almost impregnable barrier to migrating males. In order to give the possums a

Mountain pygmy-possums *are protected under state law in New South Wales and Victoria. Most of the places they live fall inside national parks near Mount Buller, Mount Bogong, Mount Higginbotham, and Kosciuszko.*

fighting chance, special tunnels have been constructed under existing roads and ski runs, providing migrating animals with alternative routes. Plans for further resorts are subject to intense scrutiny by conservation authorities. Several proposed resorts have had development permission denied on the grounds that they would be disruptive to the mountain habitat of the pygmy-possum.

Numbat

Myrmecobius fasciatus

From an all-time low of fewer than 1,000 animals in the 1970s, the numbat then began a slow recovery. However, changes in land use and the presence of many nonnative predators in Australia reduced its population again. The species will almost certainly never be as widespread as it once was.

The numbat is an unusual marsupial in many ways. It is the only living member of the group that is not even partly nocturnal, and the only one that feeds exclusively on insects. In fact, the numbat's daytime activity and its diet are interlinked. Despite its alternative names of banded or marsupial anteater, it feeds chiefly on termites, which it collects from the many tunnels and galleries that the insects create in pieces of dead wood. The termites are active during the daytime, and the numbat tailors its activity to its prey. A single numbat can consume an incredible 20,000 termites a day.

The numbat is also rather unusual looking compared with other marsupials. It is much more strikingly marked than most other marsupials, with six or seven bright white bars across its rump and a dark stripe on each side of its face. With such striking features it is hardly surprising that the numbat has won a special place in people's affections. It is now the official state animal of Western Australia.

Imported Predators

The biggest problem for the numbat, as for many other native Australian animals, has been the introduction of new predators—such as cats, dogs, and foxes—by European settlers. Research has shown that foxes have been almost entirely responsible for the numbat's decline. Two or three hundred years ago the animal was widespread throughout much of southern Australia; its range probably covered about a quarter of the continent. By the mid-1920s numbats appeared to have completely died out in South Australia, and by 1960 there were just two remnant populations in Western Australia, at Dryandra and Perup.

Quite how the two populations managed to survive in Western Australia, having died out everywhere else, is an interesting question with a simple but logical answer. The numbat used to live in almost any region where it could find termites. When the continent of Australia was invaded by introduced predators, the numbat could survive only in areas where there were both termites and secure hiding places. The best refuges for numbats are hollow logs. However, while many trees rot and fall apart, making good termite

DATA PANEL

Numbat (banded anteater, marsupial anteater, walpurti)

Myrmecobius fasciatus

Family: Myrmecobiidae

World population: Probably less than 1,000

Distribution: Southwestern Australia

Habitat: Dry, open woodlands such as eucalyptus forests

Size: Length head/body: 7–11 in (17.5–27.5 cm); tail: 5.5–6.5 in (13–17 cm). Weight: 10–20 oz (280–550 g)

Form: Distinctive-looking mammal with long, furry tail and strong, clawed feet; grayish body fur tinged red on upper back, fading to creamy gray beneath; back and rump marked with 6 or 7 striking white bars; long,

pointed muzzle, small black nose; ears erect; eyes large and black; dark stripe across sides of face and through eyes

Diet: Mostly ants and termites, plus some other insects

Breeding: Between 2 and 4 young born December–April; young spend 4 months hidden in long fur of mother's belly, attached to her teats. Independent at about 9 months. May live as long as 6 years

Related endangered species: No close relatives

Status: IUCN EN

AUSTRALIA

Western Australia

hunting grounds, only some hollow out when they die. One is the wandoo tree found in Western Australia. Fortunately for the numbat, wandoos provide plentiful hollow trunks, logs, and branches, offering both shelter and a healthy supply of termites.

Habitat Problems and Solutions

Another problem for numbats was an increase in the number of forest fires. Native people used to carefully burn small patches of vegetation each year as a means of reducing the volume of dry, inflammable material. However, when they left the land, the practice ceased. Old dead plant material accumulated, and if it caught light naturally by being struck by lightning, the resulting fires were fierce and hot. Many animals died, and the termites and their rotting logs disappeared along with them.

Clearance of land for agriculture also destroyed much good numbat habitat. In some areas trees were

The numbat is the only survivor of an entire marsupial family. Its striking coat pattern and daytime activity make it one of the more conspicuous Australian mammals.

felled for timber or fuel, leaving no deadwood at all. The campaign to save the animal has therefore taken two main approaches. One goal has been to create and preserve numbat-friendly woodland, with plenty of dead wood suitable for termites; the other has been the eradication from these areas of nonnative predators, especially foxes.

Numbats have also been reintroduced successfully into four reserves where the species had previously become extinct. There are now 400–500 animals at these reintroduction sites, in addition to 400 at Perup and 50 at Dryandra. Having populations in several areas reduces the risk that a local disaster, such as an epidemic disease or wildfire, could wipe out the entire species at a single blow.

EX

EW

CR

EN

VU

NT

LC

O

Proserpine Rock-wallaby

Petrogale persephone

A recent addition to the Australian list of scientifically described mammal species, the Proserpine rock-wallaby is in danger of disappearing before it has been fully studied. However, in this particular case of endangerment it seems that people are not entirely to blame.

The Proserpine rock-wallaby—so-named because it was found close to the town of Proserpine—has the most restricted distribution of any rock-wallaby species. Today's population appears to be all that remains of a once widespread animal. Well before people began making scientific observations of Australian wildlife, it had undergone a drastic population decline. It seems that gradual changes in climate and vegetation since the Pleistocene era (two million years ago) have not suited the species, and it has been edged out of most of its former range by two better-adapted forms: the unadorned rock-wallaby and the yellow-footed rock-wallaby. It is unfortunate for the Prosperine rock-wallaby that its last refuge happens to be in one of the fastest-developing regions of Australia.

Amazingly, given that the population lives so close to large human settlements, the Proserpine rock-wallaby was not officially recognized until 1976. Local people were aware that the wallabies existed before then, but the species is very shy and retiring, and few scientists ever got more than a fleeting glimpse as the wallabies melted into the forest or slipped quickly and quietly away over the rocks.

Habitat Pressures

Since the Proserpine rock-wallaby was formally described, a big effort has been made to study its habitat and distribution. The results are not encouraging. The populations on the mainland are small and isolated, living on tiny patches of habitat surrounded by urban development, agricultural land, or roads. This part of the Queensland coast is a rapidly expanding tourist destination. Since most of the Proserpine rock-wallaby's habitat is in private hands, there is little to

Queensland   Whitsunday Islands

AUSTRALIA

DATA PANEL

Proserpine rock-wallaby

Petrogale persephone

Family: Macropodidae

World population: Unknown

Distribution: Northeastern Queensland, Australia

Habitat: Deciduous coastal forests with grassy areas and rocky outcrops

Size: Length head/body: 19.5–25 in (50–64 cm); tail: 20–27 in (51–68 cm); male up to 50% larger than female. Weight: 9–20 lb (4–9 kg)

Form: Dog-sized animal with dark-gray fur tinged with red in places, especially around ears, face, and shoulders; white fur on chin blends with pale underside; feet and tail strikingly black

Diet: Grasses

Breeding: Single young born at any time of year; further details unknown

Related endangered species: At least 16 other species of wallaby and kangaroo, including Goodfellow's tree kangaroo (*Dendrolagus goodfellowi*) EN

Status: IUCN EN

stop it being developed one fragment at a time. It is a sad fact that most close encounters between people and Proserpine rock-wallabies are when the animals are killed in road accidents.

The Proserpine rock-wallaby is larger than most of its close relatives, but still small enough to be vulnerable to attack by dingoes and larger domestic or feral (wild) dogs. Domestic cats may also pose a threat, not because they hunt the wallabies, but because they carry a disease called toxoplasmosis, which may affect wallabies as well. The combined effect of the threats, added to the original problem of competition with other wallaby species, adds up to a grim outlook for the Proserpine rock-wallaby, especially on the Australian mainland.

There are, however, small additional populations of the endangered Proserpine rock-wallaby in several nearby parks, some of which—including Dryander and Conway national parks—and on Gloucester Island. While the colonies are still highly vulnerable on account of their small size, the parks are free of predators and protected from development. It seems that the parks will soon provide the only secure refuge for the species, which may otherwise be destined for extinction.

In the future the small wild populations on the mainland and the various island refuges could be boosted by the reintroduction of captive-bred individuals. The wallabies could in time be relocated to other island habitats from which predators and competing species have been removed. Such intervention may give the species a fighting chance.

The Proserpine rock-wallaby *is larger than most of its closely related competitors. Even so, it seems to have been losing the battle for habitat gradually over several thousand years.*

Archbold's Bowerbird

Archboldia papuensis

Unknown to science before 1939, Archbold's bowerbird remains one of the most elusive and enigmatic of forest birds. No one knows how many there are, but we do know that its native forests are being steadily destroyed and that its long-term survival is in question.

Archbold's bowerbird inhabits the remote and mysterious mountain forests of New Guinea. The forests are home to some of the most extraordinary birds in the world, including the spectacular birds of paradise that are famous for their fabulous plumage and breathtaking courtship displays.

Through competing with each other to attract potential mates, male birds of paradise have evolved into creatures of incomparable beauty, but at a cost. Their adornments are conspicuous and cumbersome, making them tempting targets for predators. It is perhaps no surprise that some bowerbirds, including Archbold's, have developed a courtship strategy that makes eye-catching plumage unnecessary.

Master Builders

Instead of flaunting his beauty at a potential mate, the male Archbold's bowerbird dazzles the female with a demonstration of his artistic skill. He builds a bower (arbor), which has the appearance of a decorated dance floor, then calls and displays until a female comes to inspect his work. If she is sufficiently impressed, she mates with him, then leaves to raise a brood while he advertizes for another female. The best builders mate with the most females, and over time competition between males has developed the building skills of some bowerbirds to an astonishing degree: The ornamented bower of one species, the Vogelkop bowerbird, is the most elaborate structure built by any animal except humans.

Although the bower of the Archbold male is not in quite the same league as that of the Vogelkop bowerbird, it is still an impressive production. The male selects an area of forest floor overhung by low branches, clears about 40 to 65 square feet (4 to 6 sq. m), and creates a mat of dry ferns, fronds, and moss. He decorates the edges of the mat with trinkets, including piles of black beetle wing cases, blue-black and gray snail shells, blue berries, and chips of amber resin from tree ferns, sometimes adding the plume of a King of Saxony bird of paradise as a final flourish. He then gathers orchid

DATA PANEL

Archbold's bowerbird

Archboldia papuensis

Family: Ptilonorhynchidae

World population: Unknown

Distribution: Central mountain ranges of New Guinea, mainly above 6,500 ft (2,000 m); sometimes as low as 5,600 ft (1,750 m)

Habitat: Mossy mountain forest with southern beech, Pandanus palm, tree ferns, and dense stands of bamboo

Size: Length: 14.5 in (37 cm)

Form: Large, jaylike bird with a short, stout bill. Male black with bright-yellow crest extending from forehead to neck; female dull black with ocher markings on wing primaries; juvenile male grayish with no yellow crest

Diet: Mainly fruit; also buds, flowers, seeds, succulent stems, and leaves; a few small animals

Breeding: Male is promiscuously polygamous, attracting females to mate by displaying and calling from his bower or display mat. Mated female builds a cup nest in a tree, incubating eggs and rearing young alone

Related endangered species: Fire-maned bowerbird (*Sericulus bakeri*) NT. Two other species in the bowerbird family, the tooth-billed bowerbird (*Scenopoeetes dentirostris*) and the golden-fronted bowerbird (*Amblyornis flavifrons*), were classified by the IUCN as LRnt, but have since been removed from the list

Status: IUCN NT

vines from the forest trees and drapes them from the overhanging branches to create ground-sweeping curtains around and across the mat. His stage set, he begins his performance.

Calling with a selection of whistles, growls, and hoarse cries, he attracts a female, who usually perches on one of the overhanging branches. He then starts a strange begging, groveling display, crawling across the mat with his body and tail pressed to the ground, holding his wings partly open and churring almost continuously. Meanwhile, the female hops from perch to perch, fluttering coquettishly over his head so he has to chase her around the mat. This pursuit may be the female's way of assessing the male's fitness; if he passes the test, she mates with him.

Lonely Isolation

Archbold's bowerbird lives only in the higher mountain forests of New Guinea, mainly at over 6,500 feet (1,980 m) above sea level. At such altitudes the forests are cold, misty, and damp, and the branches are festooned with epiphytic mosses (those that grow on the surface of other plants), as well as lichens, ferns, and orchids. It is a very different habitat from the lowland rain forests, and the animals that live there are so adapted to the highland conditions that they never stray down to the valleys between the mountain ridges. As a result, local populations of Archbold's bowerbird are effectively isolated on "islands" of highland habitat.

Shrinking Forest

Archbold's bowerbird is patchily distributed in the central ranges of the island, and local populations in the east are found in a small range of just 300 square miles (800 sq. km). Within this area the birds are threatened by logging in two of their forest strongholds, and as their habitats contract, the birds may soon be in trouble. Elsewhere on the island local populations seem to be larger, and their habitats are still intact, but this situation may not last.

Conservationists are concerned for the future of Archbold's bowerbird. Formerly classed as Vulnerable, it is now considered to be Near Threatened. Its IUCN classification is a clear warning that if habitat destruction from logging continues at the present rate, the bird may soon join the danger list, along with many of its unique neighbors in the mountain forests of New Guinea.

A male Archbold's bowerbird *attracts female mates by his prowess at building a decorative bower, rather than by his plumage.*

Bali Starling

Leucopsar rothschildi

The beautiful Bali starling's tiny surviving population is confined to a minute area of a national park. For over 70 years large numbers have been taken from the wild to supply the international cage-bird trade, a threat that could still result in its extinction.

The Bali starling is the only bird species to be found exclusively on the Indonesian island of Bali. It has probably always been restricted to the northwestern third of this small island and was probably already very scarce when first discovered in the early 1900s. The population of the Bali starling has been greatly reduced over the last century by relentless trapping for the worldwide cage-bird trade, and increasing habitat loss has been an important secondary threat. As a result, it is now one of the world's rarest and most threatened birds.

DATA PANEL

Bali starling

Leucopsar rothschildi

Family: Sturnidae

World population: More than 100 birds in 2009, 50 at Bali Barat and 65 introduced on Nusa Penida island

Distribution: Endemic to the island of Bali, Indonesia. Confined to Bali Barat National Park, northwestern Bali

Habitat: During the breeding season open shrubland and savanna with many trees, including palms, and adjacent tropical moist deciduous monsoon forest below an altitude of 575 ft (175 m); at other times disperses to the edges of the forest and flooded savanna woodland

Size: Length: 10 in (25 cm). Weight: 3–3.2 oz (85–90 g)

Form: Plump, thrush-sized bird. Whole body has white plumage; bright-blue bare skin around each eye tapers to a point; has a long crest, especially in males, that the bird can erect; tail and wings white with black tips; strong gray or brown bill and pale blue-gray legs

Diet: Caterpillars, termites, ants, and other insects; also seeds and fruit

Breeding: October–November; nests in tree holes, often old woodpecker nesting holes lined by male with dry twigs; female incubates 2–3 pale-blue eggs for 12–14 days; young fledge in about 3 weeks

Related endangered species: Black-winged starling (*Sturnus melanopterus*) CR; white-faced starling (*S. albofrontatus*) VU; Pohnpei mountain starling (*Aplonis pelzelni*) CR; white-eyed starling (*A. brunneicapilla*) EN

Status: IUCN CR

In Great Demand

The dazzling white plumage, a contrasting patch of bare, bright-blue skin around the face, and a luxuriant crest ensure that the Bali starling is highly sought after by bird collectors. In 1928, less than 20 years after the species became known in the West, the first Bali starlings were being exported to Europe, and they first bred in captivity three years later. Over succeeding decades the collectors' demands for wild-caught individuals of the beautiful birds grew—despite the fact that they proved easy to breed in captivity. During the 1960s and 1970s the cage-bird trade in Bali starlings was vigorous, and many hundreds of birds were caught to be exported overseas. The trade in the Bali starling continues today, despite the fact that it was placed on Appendix I of CITES in 1970, has been protected under Indonesian law since 1971, and the species' entire population occurs in a national park where it is the subject of a special conservation program. As numbers have dwindled, owning a Bali starling has become a sign of prestige to some collectors. In the mid-1990s a single bird could fetch $2,000 on the black market.

Today most birds are sold to collectors in Indonesia, where many people keep cage birds. Methods of capture involve smearing sticky "bird lime" on branches to glue unsuspecting birds when they land; using a tethered bird as a decoy; or raiding nests at night. Recently, poachers have equipped themselves with telescopes, walkie-talkies, and fine-mesh mist nets to help entrap the starlings.

Borneo

INDONESIA

Java

Bali

Bali Barat National Park

Sumbawa

Serious Setbacks

Although the primary threat to the Bali starling is from illegal trapping, the dwindling population is placed at further risk by long-term destruction of its habitat. Unlike other restricted-range birds in Java and Bali that are found in rain forest at higher altitudes, the Bali starling prefers drier, more open lowland, deciduous monsoon forest, and densely wooded savanna with an understory of grasses. During the early 20th century such areas were mainly undisturbed, but the spread and growth of settlements have destroyed much of the species' habitat. With fertile volcanic soil, the islands of Bali and Java support some of the world's most intensive agriculture—and about 60 percent of the human population of Indonesia.

Of an original area of 1,370 square miles (3,550 sq. km) of monsoon forest, only an eighth is left. Much has been converted to plantations of kapok and coconut trees and for settlements. Even in the Bali Barat reserve—to which the birds have been confined since the early 1980s—about a third of the 38 square miles (100 sq. km) of suitable habitat has been converted into plantations and settlements. Other threats to the park include tourism.

Alarming Decline

The Bali starling largely disappeared from the southern part of its range during the 1960s and from the northeastern part in the 1970s. Until 1974 the lack of research into the bird life of Indonesia meant that no one knew how many Bali starlings remained. The first census produced an estimate of 100 birds before the breeding season. Through the late 1970s and early 1980s counts suggested there were about 200 birds, but by 1989 there were just 28—largely as a result of poaching. The alarming decline continued until 1990, when there were just 15 birds in the wild. At this time, prices on the black market reached $2,000 per bird.

A conservation program was launched in 1983 involving the Indonesian government, BirdLife International, and several other agencies. It helped strengthen protection of the birds in Bali Barat National Park, where all the remaining wild birds were, and achieved major advances in techniques for releasing captive-bred birds. More recently, in 2011, a captive-breeding center was opened; birds are bred, then released into the wild. However, the program has not removed the threat of extinction because numbers are still very small. The few wild birds left may face additional threats, including native predators, disease, competition with other birds, and the effects of climate change in long periods of drought.

The Bali starling
is still being poached for the cage-bird trade, despite protective legislation.

Black Stilt

Himantopus novaezelandiae

With a wild population of fewer than 100 individuals, the distinctive black stilt of New Zealand is one of the rarest of all the world's birds. This is despite 30 years of effort by conservationists to make good its losses to habitat destruction, introduced predators, and interbreeding with other species.

The black stilt is the only globally threatened member of its family, the stilts and avocets. Until the late 19th century it was a common and widespread breeder in New Zealand. By the turn of the century the black stilt nested only on South Island. Within another 30 years nests could be found only on inland riverbeds and associated wetlands in the lowland parts of southern Canterbury and central Otago regions and the Mackenzie Basin.

By 1940 the total population was down to an estimated 500 to 1,000 individuals. The real crash, however, began in the early 1950s, when numbers plummeted; just 23 birds were left by 1981, all of them breeding in the Mackenzie Basin. Today black stilts nest only along rivers in the upper Waitaki Valley. Of the total population only 40 are breeding adults.

After breeding most of the birds move short distances to ponds or lakes before wintering on nearby river deltas around large lakes, although a few migrate to the northern harbors of North Island.

Introduced Predators

The major cause of the black stilt's decline has been the introduction by human settlers of nonnative predators. In a land with no natural mammalian predators the stilts had evolved no antipredator behavior, and proved easy targets for invading cats, ferrets, weasels, stoats, brown rats, and hedgehogs. Mammals such as rabbits provided a new food source for native bird predators, notably Australasian harriers and kelp gulls, increasing their numbers and so putting extra pressure on the stilts.

In addition to their fearlessness of predators the

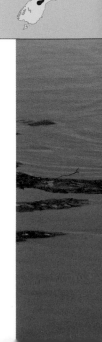

North Island

NEW ZEALAND

South Island

DATA PANEL

Black stilt

Himantopus novaezelandiae

Family: Recurvirostridae

World population: 130 birds in 2012

Distribution: New Zealand; entire population now breeds only in upper Waitaki Valley, South Island, although small numbers migrate to winter on North Island

Habitat: Breeds on the banks of intertwining rivers and side streams; also occurs in swamps and other wetlands

Size: Length: 14.5–15.8 in (37–40 cm). Weight: about 7.8 oz (220 g)

Form: Elegant wader with long, thin, black bill and long, pinkish-red legs; plumage entirely black with greenish gloss to back and wings; female has shorter legs on average; nonbreeding adults may show grayish or whitish forehead and chin; juveniles have white head, neck, and breast, becoming progressively darker

Diet: Chiefly small aquatic invertebrates; also small fish

Breeding: September–January, usually solitary; both sexes build a nest near water; nest is a shallow scrape that is often well lined with vegetation; usually 4 greenish eggs with dark-brown or blackish blotches and streaks are laid; incubation by both sexes for 3–4 weeks; fledging period 4–8 weeks

Related endangered species: No other species in the stilt and avocet family

Status: IUCN CR

stilts have other traits that make them vulnerable: They nest as solitary pairs on banks that are accessible to predators, and the young remain flightless for a long period—up to eight weeks.

Habitat Loss and Hybridization

Another factor affecting the stilt is habitat destruction and alteration. Many of New Zealand's swamps and other wetlands have been drained over the past few hundred years. The process continues today in the birds' last refuge in the Mackenzie Basin. Another threat comes from hydroelectric power projects, which have also dramatically modified the habitat. Reduced flows in rivers have allowed predators to reach nesting islands more easily, while floods destroy nests. Habitat changes have also affected the stilts' feeding areas. The result is that the stilts have been forced to abandon sites by water for drier areas where they are more likely to suffer plundering by predators.

Also, introduced plants, such as lupins and willows, have quickly spread along rivers, replacing native vegetation and making the habitat unsuitable for the black stilts.

As the numbers of black stilts declined, their populations became fragmented. The birds became so widely separated from one another that there were often too few of them on a particular stretch of river for all the adults to find mates. At the same time, the other stilt species in New Zealand, the pied stilts, were becoming more abundant. Because the geographical separation of the two species was fairly recent, black stilts had not evolved sufficiently different courtship rituals to prevent interbreeding, which reduced the species' numbers further.

Reversing the Decline

Conservationists have tried to reduce predation by trapping predators around the nests or fencing off nest sites. Other aims are to establish a self-sustaining population on a suitable predator-free island and to raise public awareness about the bird. However, it is the captive-breeding program (which began in 1979) that has been primarily responsible for the increase in numbers. Young captive-reared birds are released every year: 80 in 2009 and 70 in 2012, for example. In 2012, before the release of captive-bred birds, the free-living population was about 130 individuals.

The black stilt's *long legs enable it to wade into relatively deep water to feed. It uses its long, needlelike bill to snap up mayflies, caddisflies, stoneflies and their larvae, other invertebrates, and even small fish.*

Night Parrot

Geopsittacus occidentalis

A relative of the budgerigar, the night parrot of the Australian Outback is one of the world's least-known and most rarely seen birds. It is assumed to have a tiny population, and its range is unknown. Although sightings have become rarer, it may not be currently declining.

The unusual night parrot has always been shrouded in mystery. Although it was described by observers as common in parts of South Australia during the 1870s and 1880s, it seems even then to have been extremely elusive. Since that time there have been only a handful of authenticated records, with most sightings remaining unconfirmed. In fact, until very recently the species was thought to be possibly extinct.

Despite two publicity campaigns and at least five dedicated searches for night parrots, there were no authenticated sightings between October 17 1990, in the Mount Isa Uplands, 22 miles (36 km) south of the settlement of Boulia in northwestern Queensland, and 2005 when three birds were seen in the Pilbara region of Western Australia. In 2006, a dead juvenile was found in Diamantina National Park, Queensland.

Nocturnal Habits

One of the problems facing those searching for the night parrot is suggested by its common name, since, unusually for a parrot, it is nocturnal in its habits. (The only other habitually nocturnal parrot is the kakapo of New Zealand.) Historical accounts refer to the bird roosting during the day among shrubs, under dense clumps of spinifex grass, even in caves or in tunnels that it dug into the sandy desert soil. The birds were reported to leave their roosts late in the evening, either singly, in pairs, or in small groups, in order to visit the nearest water source before feeding. They would then usually return to water several more times in the course of the night.

The parrot's dark, barred plumage has always made it hard to spot—a problem compounded by the bird's reaction when disturbed. Instead of taking flight, it prefers to run. Even when pursued closely, it flies for only a short distance a few feet off the ground before diving into dense vegetation and running off at right angles to its line of flight to be quickly lost from view. Because of the difficulty of getting more than a glimpse of the furtive bird, some claimed reports may in fact be

DATA PANEL

Night parrot

Geopsittacus occidentalis

Family: Psittacidae

World population: Difficult to estimate but probably 50–250 birds

Distribution: Australian Outback

Habitat: Arid and semiarid plains; spinifex grassland or goosefoot and samphire shrublands on floodplains, claypans, or by watercourses or salt lakes; recently in rolling plains of Mitchell grass with scattered goosefoot shrubs

Size: Length: 8.5–10 in (22–25 cm); wingspan: 17–18 in (44–46 cm)

Form: Smallish parrot with stocky build and short tail. Bright yellowish-green below breast with dark mottling and barring except on belly; upper wing has dark-grayish flight feathers and pale-yellow wingbar; underwing grayish-green with broader yellow wingbar; tail browner

Diet: Reported to feed on seeds of grasses and other plants

Breeding: Virtually unknown; nests described as being of small sticks or leaves in clump of vegetation at end of tunnel or runway made in soil; clutch may be 2–4 eggs, possibly up to 6

Related endangered species: Eleven in the subfamily Platycercinae to which the night parrot belongs, including golden-shouldered parrot (*Psephotus chrysopterygius*) EN; swift parrot (*Lathamus discolor*) EN; and orange-bellied parrot (*Neophema chrysogaster*) CR

Status: IUCN EN

range and population (not illustration) AUSTRALIA

mistaken sightings of other parrots. The ground parrot, its closest relative, is superficially similar in appearance, although it has a longer tail and a different range and habitat. In contrast, another relative, the budgerigar, could hardly be more different, being abundant in many parts of Australia and also known around the world as a cage bird. The budgerigar is distinctly smaller, however, and active by day.

There have been unconfirmed reports of night parrot sightings from all the mainland states of Australia and from the Northern Territory, so it is possible that the bird survives at low densities over much of its former range in the arid and semiarid regions of the Outback. This vast area covers more than 1 million square miles (2.6 million sq. km), helping to explain why the bird is so hard to find.

Although there is too little information available at present to allow for any clear estimate of the parrot's numbers, the scarcity of recorded sightings over the past 120 years almost certainly reflects a real decline in its abundance. However, the fact that sightings in recent years have come from locations very far apart suggests a bigger population than had been feared. Consequently, the species is no longer considered to have Critically Endangered status.

Likely Threats

In the absence of hard evidence, the threats thought most likely to endanger the ground-nesting night parrot include predation by nonnative mammals, especially wild cats and foxes. An early report of the parrot's disappearance from Innaminka Station, South Australia, in the 1880s coincided with the introduction of large numbers of cats from New South Wales. The birds may also suffer competition for food from cattle and other livestock. Rabbits are another source of competition for night parrots, eating their food and damaging their habitat. Also, the birds' water supplies may have been reduced by the spread of wild camels.

There is an urgent need to find the remaining birds; the species could then be helped by captive-breeding programs, using techniques developed for ground parrots. Once a site is found to contain night parrots, other targets will include researching the birds' ecology, controlling threats from predators, and reversing the damage caused by habitat degradation.

The night parrot *is unusual not just in its nocturnal habits that have given it its name, but also for its ground-nesting behavior.*

Salmon-crested Cockatoo

Cacatua moluccensis

The beautiful salmon-crested cockatoo has lost much of its prime habitat on the beautiful Indonesian islands of Seram and Ambon as a result of logging. It is a sought-after species for the flourishing cage-bird trade; trapping now poses an even greater threat to its continued survival.

In the wild the salmon-crested cockatoo is found today only on the large, mountainous island of Seram in the eastern part of Indonesia and at a site on Ambon, one of Seram's three offshore islands. It also once occured on Saparua and Haruku. All these islands are part of the South Moluccas (Maluku) island group, and the handsome crested bird is often known as the Moluccan or Seram cockatoo.

Until the late 1970s the salmon-crested cockatoo was common over most of its range, feeding and roosting in flocks of up to 16 birds—except in the breeding season. Nowadays, it survives in much smaller numbers and has been driven out of many of its former haunts in the primary rain forest by extensive logging. Although some birds have been recorded in recently logged areas, they occur at a far lower density than in primary habitat.

Popular Cage Bird

The salmon-crested cockatoo also has the misfortune of being one of the most highly sought after of all cage birds. In 1982 more than 6,400 were trapped; they accounted for 15 percent of all birds captured on Seram for the international cage-bird trade. The species was extinct over most of its former range by 1985. More than 74,000 birds were exported from Indonesia between 1981 and 1990. In 1989 its situation was regarded as so serious that the cockatoo was listed by CITES; all trade in the bird was banned.

Since 1987 the government of Indonesia has banned exports, but the law is often flouted and birds are still trapped. The trappers sell the cockatoos to dealers, who sell the birds to smugglers. The birds are stuffed into plastic pipes and concealed in suitcases, then sent by air to collectors and unscrupulous pet shops worldwide.

The trappers from local villages risk their lives by climbing 200-foot- (60-m)- high trees to net the cockatoos at their nest entrances or to snare them in fishing lines. For their efforts they receive just a few dollars for each bird. By the time one of their catches has reached a dealer in the United States or elsewhere, it will be sold for thousands of dollars—that is, if the bird survives

DATA PANEL

Salmon-crested cockatoo

Cacatua moluccensis

Family: Psittacidae

World population: More than 10,000 birds in the wild

Distribution: The Indonesian islands of Seram and Ambon; until recently also on Saparua and Haruku

Habitat: Forests and open woodland, from sea level to 3,300 ft (1,000 m)

Size: Length: 18–20 in (46–52 cm)

Form: Usually pale salmon pink, sometimes white; large, backward-curving crest with deep-pink central feathers; underwings mostly deep salmon pink; undertail orange pink; female slightly larger than male

Diet: Seeds, fruit, berries, and nuts; green coconuts in plantations

Breeding: Little known to scientists. Nests in tree hollows, often enlarged to 15 ft (4.5 m) with use of powerful bill. In captivity, known to lay 2 eggs at a time; incubates eggs for 4 weeks; chicks have sparse, yellow down and stay in nest for about 4 months

Related endangered species: Philippine cockatoo (*Cacatua haematuropygia*) CR; yellow-crested cockatoo (*C. sulphurea*) CR; white cockatoo (*C. alba*) VU; Tanimbar cockatoo (*C. goffini*) NT

Status: IUCN VU

The plumage of the salmon-crested cockatoo *is a delicate pink. The bird also has a backward-curving salmon-pink and white crest that it raises during courtship.*

the journey. Most die of starvation, dehydration, suffocation, or disease in transit. Even if they do survive, they may be impossible to keep as pets, since wild-caught cockatoos often pluck their plumage bare, bite holes in their skin, or chew through their perches or their owner's furniture.

Prospects for the Future

There is hope for the future: The California-based project Bird Watch, working with BirdLife International, has initiated a program of research, conservation, and education. It has helped two Seram villages build a rain-forest canopy viewing platform enabling tourists to watch birds and other wildlife. Each tourist pays a small amount of money, plus fees to local guides—as much as a logging company was offering for cutting down a single tree. The villagers decided to pull out of the contract with the loggers that would have cleared the cockatoo's habitat. Other initiatives—including a bird-adoption project—are also planned. Such measures have helped raise awareness of the plight of this beautiful cockatoo.

The salmon-crested cockatoo breeds well in captivity. Encouraging responsible aviculture (the raising and care of birds in captivity) is an important means of reducing the pressure exerted by bird trapping on the wild population. There is a sizable stock for captive breeding, including more than 300 birds in zoos worldwide and more than 10,000 in private collections.

EX
EW
CR
EN
VU
NT
LC
O

Southern Cassowary

Casuarius casuarius

The huge, flightless southern cassowary is among the largest of all bird species. With continuing concerted conservation efforts—including habitat protection, the control of predators, and the reduction of disease—the southern cassowary's future may be safeguarded.

The southern cassowary is the largest land animal in New Guinea. It is one of three similar species of large, flightless birds on the island, but the only one that is also found in Australia. Populations of southern cassowary in Australia have declined by more than 20 percent over 30 years. An estimated total of 2,500 birds in 13 subpopulations remain in the rain forests of coastal northeastern Queensland, in part of the remote, sparsely populated Cape York Peninsula, and farther south in an area between Cooktown and Townsville. In New Guinea the species is more widespread and occurs throughout most of the lowlands. Nonetheless, it may have experienced large declines here as well.

Distinctive Features

Along with its highly modified feathers that are like luxuriant mammal hair, a distinctive feature of the southern cassowary is the blade-shaped protuberance (casque) on the top of the head. There are several theories about the casque's function. It is most likely that, along with the bare skin and wattles (loose folds of skin hanging from the neck), it plays a vital role in social behavior. Perhaps the most unlikely theory is that the bird uses it to hack through jungle vegetation. Captive individuals have been seen to use the casque as a shovel; in the wild the birds may use it to move leaf litter when searching for food.

Cassowaries have long had great cultural importance for the forest tribes of New Guinea, featuring in their legends and mystical rituals. As well as hunting them for their meat, the people use their feathers for ceremonial headdresses, make the quills of their primary wing feathers into earrings or nosepins, and carve the leg bones into daggers, spoons, or other implements. Villagers often keep the birds in captivity, taking them as chicks and feeding them until they are large enough to provide a substantial meal or to sell to a trader. As soon as they reach adulthood, if not before, the birds are securely penned.

DATA PANEL

Southern cassowary (double-wattled, two-wattled, common, or Australian cassowary)

Casuarius casuarius

Family: Casuariidae

World population: 10,000–20,000 individuals

Distribution: New Guinea, both in Papua (formerly Irian Jaya), Indonesia, and Papua New Guinea, as well as Indonesian islands of Aru and Seram; parts of northeastern Australia

Habitat: Rain forests, fruit plantations, savanna, and mangroves near forest

Size: Height: up to 5.5 ft (1.7 m). Weight: male 64–75 lb (29–34 kg); female 128 lb (58 kg)

Form: Heavy-bodied, flightless bird covered with glossy, black, hairlike plumage. Primary wingtip feathers—modified as strong, bare quills—curve under body, head, and neck. Pale-blue bare skin on head, darker blue on neck with variable red areas; 2 fleshy red wattles hang from foreneck. Casque protrudes from top of head; female has brighter bare areas and bigger casque; bare parts vary in color with mood. Chicks have yellow and black stripes; immatures brown with smaller casque and wattles

Diet: Mainly fruit; also fungi, snails, insects and other invertebrates; sometimes small vertebrates or carrion

Breeding: After mating, female spends a few weeks with male in his territory; 3–5 dark-green eggs laid in shallow nest built by male. Female mates with other males, leaving each in turn to incubate eggs alone for about 7 weeks; male cares for chicks for about 9 months

Related endangered species: Dwarf cassowary (*Casuarius bennetti*) NT; northern cassowary (*C. unappendiculatus*) VU

Status: IUCN VU

New Guinea

INDONESIA

PAPUA NEW GUINEA

AUSTRALIA

Although they prefer to escape from danger by running away—their powerful legs and feet enable them to move at up to 30 miles per hour (48 km/h)—cassowaries can be dangerous when defending young or when cornered, as sometimes happens with captive birds. The innermost toe on each foot bears a razor-sharp, daggerlike claw measuring 4 inches (10 cm). The cassowary uses the claw as a formidable weapon.

Threats

Hunting poses a significant threat to the southern cassowary in New Guinea, although populations can remain viable where the birds are regularly trapped. As well as destroying habitat, logging has opened up new areas to hunters. In Australia the main threat was, until recently, the rapid destruction of areas of rain forest. The remaining subpopulations are isolated by the fragmentation of their habitat and are vulnerable to being hit by vehicles as they cross roads. The birds are also at risk from disease, hunting (to protect crops or for food and sport), and predation by dogs (and perhaps pigs). The pigs may also compete with the birds for food or degrade their habitat.

Conservation

Conservationists have set targets for the protection of the southern cassowary in both Papua and Papua New Guinea. They include monitoring populations, analyzing the effects of hunting and logging on numbers, and encouraging communities to restrict the number that they kill each year.

In Australia similar initiatives exist, and most cassowary habitat is now protected by law. There is still a need to improve monitoring techniques and to research population dynamics. The priorities are the control of predators, the prevention of habitat destruction and disease, and the reduction of road deaths. Fortunately, the destruction of rain forests in Australia has almost stopped, while in New Guinea there are still large areas that are as yet unaffected by hunting or habitat destruction.

The southern cassowary *has powerful legs and feet, enabling it to run very fast. The bladelike casque on top of the head is another distinctive feature of this flightless bird.*

Victoria Crowned Pigeon

Goura victoria

Among the largest of all the world's pigeons, the Victoria crowned pigeon is threatened by hunting for food and feathers. The birds are especially vulnerable since they are remarkably tame.

The Victoria crowned pigeon is one of three very closely related species of giant pigeon found on the island of New Guinea; the other two are the southern crowned pigeon and the western crowned pigeon. True to their names, the birds have a "crown"—a fanlike crest of lacy feathers.

The Victoria crowned pigeon occurs in both Papua, a province of Indonesia, and Papua New Guinea, as well as on the Indonesian islands of Biak-Supiori (where it may have been introduced) and Yapen. It breeds with the western and southern crowned pigeons in places where they occur together in the northwest of the island. The reason for its absence between Astrolabe Bay and Collingwood Bay is not known. It could be that it has never occurred there, or that it did but has been wiped out at some time in the past.

Prized as Food

As plump as a turkey, the Victoria crowned pigeon has long been prized as food by local hunters, since each bird provides plenty of succulent meat. The birds are hunted, and young are taken from the nests to rear for food. Some birds are also still killed for their beautiful crown feathers, which are used in traditional headdresses. Trapping of the birds for the aviary trade may also pose a significant threat.

From Bows to Rifles

From With modern firearms replacing the bow and arrow and the snare, the birds are much easier to kill, although their tameness is legendary—at least in regions where they have not been heavily exploited. When approached, a pigeon will often run away. If it does not make good its escape that way, it flies up with a loud beating of its broad wings to perch awkwardly on a nearby low branch of a tree in the forest understory, peering with curiosity at its pursuer. Such a large, static target is not difficult to hit.

DATA PANEL

Victoria crowned pigeon (Victoria goura, white-tipped goura/crowned pigeon)

Goura victoria

Family: Columbidae

World population: 2,500–10,000 birds

Distribution: Parts of northern New Guinea (in both Papua and Papua New Guinea); islands of Biak-Supiori and Yapen

Habitat: Lowland forest, mainly at lowest altitudes

Size: Length: 29 in (74 cm)

Form: Huge, plump pigeon with large crest of white-tipped feathers; plumage generally bluish gray with broad, pale-gray bar in front of narrow, dark-maroon bar on each wing; pale-gray band at end of tail; large maroon area on breast; eyes have red irises; bill dark gray, paler at tip; legs and feet purplish red

Diet: Mainly berries and other fruit; seeds that have fallen to the ground

Breeding: Builds a neat, compact nest of stems, leaves, and sticks; birds in captivity begin breeding from the age of 15 months; lays single white egg and cares for fledgling for several months after hatching

Related endangered species: Western crowned pigeon *(Goura cristata)* VU; southern crowned pigeon *(G. scheepmakeri)* VU

Status: IUCN VU

Threats from Logging

Victoria crowned pigeons are exclusively forest dwellers. Although they have sometimes been found as high up as 1,970 feet (600 m), they prefer forests at much lower altitudes, particularly those on flat terrain. Unfortunately, these are often just the type of forests that are threatened by logging. As well as causing immediate damage to the pigeons' forest habitat, the building of roads into the forests for logging vehicles also helps hunters gain access to the areas where the birds live.

Cause for Concern

Hunting has wiped out local populations around some villages, with birds surviving only in remote forests. In some places in Papua where settlers have moved in from other places, the species has disappeared from areas where it had previously survived regular hunting by the local people.

Although the size of its population is unknown, the Victoria crowned pigeon has been given Vulnerable status by the IUCN because conservationists think that it may be relatively rare and is declining rapidly, largely as a result of hunting. However, the Victoria crowned pigeon remains common in some more remote, undisturbed areas of forest. New information on its population size and the success of future conservation initiatives will perhaps enable its Vulnerable status to be revised.

The species is protected by law in Papua

New Guinea. There are plans for various research and education programs, which will include making people aware of the need to reduce hunting. Other aims are to establish new protected areas in lowland forests and to enforce protection in those areas that are already set aside as reserves.

The Victoria crowned pigeon *has sturdy legs and feet adapted for a life spent mainly on the ground. However, the birds can fly well and perch and roost in trees.*

Fijian Crested Iguana

Brachylophus vitiensis

Discovered in 1979, the Fijian crested iguana is one of the world's rarest iguanas. Regarded as sacred by some Fijians but evil by others, its main survival obstacle is disappearing habitat.

Hidden away in just a handful of the 800 small islands that make up the state of Fiji, the Fijian crested iguana was only discovered in 1979. Some islanders refer to iguanas as *saumuri*, others call them *vokai*. Attitudes toward them also differ; the animals are considered sacred to some groups but evil to others. It is taboo even to mention them on certain islands; on others they must not be mentioned in the hearing of women. Some Fijians fear the iguanas, believing that their tail has a venomous tip and that they launch themselves at intruders and can only be gotten off by using fire or saltwater. The belief may stem from the female's aggressive behavior when defending her nest.

The Fijian crested iguana is an attractive lizard, but when threatened, it turns black—another cause of islanders' superstition. The animal is thought to resemble more closely the ancestral form that had reached the islands millions of years ago, probably by "rafting" on large masses of vegetation wrenched loose in South America by fierce storms. This is now generally accepted as the means by which the islands (which were never part of any continent) were colonized by reptiles and other land creatures.

Competition from Goats—and Other Threats

The main Fijian crested iguana population is on Yaduataba Island. When first discovered, they shared the island with a similar number of goats, which had been given to the islanders to provide a source of income from trading them. One of the main iguana foods is the vau tree, which is also enjoyed by goats. On the island of Monuriki only 12 iguanas survived: The goats had eaten most of the vegetation, apart from the tall trees. The iguanas on Monuriki were all adults; the young had probably starved to death as a result of the goats' activities. The goats were removed and Yaduataba declared a reserve in 1981; without this action the iguanas would have died out.

Like other animals in restricted habitats, the Fijian iguanas have been affected by logging and predation by cats and dogs. Small islands are also vulnerable to hurricanes and further expansion of the human population.

Unlike the common green iguanas, which lay up to 40 eggs per clutch, Fijian iguanas lay small clutches, and not all the eggs hatch. Reduced fertility is often the result of inbreeding and is

DATA PANEL

Fijian crested iguana

Brachylophus vitiensis

Family: Iguanidae

World population: At least 12,700

Distribution: Yaduataba Island, Fiji

Habitat: Shoreline forests on uninhabited islands

Size: Length: 36 in (90 cm)

Form: Dark green in color with narrow white stripes on the body, tail, and legs; a row of spines along the back; yellowish tinge around the lips and nostrils; belly mottled with green and cream. Large dewlap (loose fold of skin hanging beneath the throat)

Diet: Vau tree and other vegetation

Breeding: One clutch of 4 eggs that hatch within 6–7 months

Related endangered species: Fijian banded iguana (*Brachylophus fasciatus*) CR

Status: IUCN CR

Vanua Levu
Yaduataba
Taveuni
Mamanuca
Group
FIJI
Lau Group
Viti Levu
Kadavu

a problem that often occurs in relatively small island populations. The Fijian crested iguana's eggs also take much longer to hatch than those of other iguanas.

Conservation

Taronga Zoo in New South Wales in Australia had already run a successful captive-management plan for Fijian banded iguanas, and the animals had been released back into the wild; wild populations were also on the increase in Fiji and Tonga. In 1997, in view of the apparent recovery, the authorities in Fiji decided to send the captive specimens to other zoos and to concentrate efforts on the crested iguana. The International Conservation Fund for the Fijian Crested Iguana (ICFFCI) was set up to organize conservation.

According to a recent survey an estimated 12,700 crested iguanas now live on Yaduataba; the island's area is only about 173 acres (70 ha). The survey was difficult to conduct because Fijian crested iguanas are secretive and well camouflaged, so much of the research was done at night using lamps to spot the sleeping animals in the trees. The iguanas' faeces have also been studied to figure out which plants they eat. This is important for habitat restoration, particularly if other islands will eventually be used for releases.

Thanks to the ICFFCI a captive-breeding program for the crested iguana has been set up at Kula Eco Park in Fiji, with Taronga Zoo providing veterinary assistance and management expertise. Young crested iguanas have already been hatched and will be kept as a "reservoir population." There are also plans to restore the wild habitat. Raising awareness and support among islanders for the conservation effort are important. Books in the Fijian language have been distributed to schools. The Kula Eco Park runs school visits in which the need for conservation is promoted, and children can see and handle the iguanas.

The Fijian crested iguana's *future looks more promising than it did when first discovered, but its small habitats are still vulnerable.*

Tuatara

Sphenodon punctatus

The tuatara is a unique lizardlike reptile and the sole surviving member of a group common in Mesozoic times. Now one of the rarest reptiles in the world, it is struggling to survive on small islands off the coast of New Zealand.

In spite of their appearance, tuataras are not lizards. Sometimes referred to as "living fossils" because they have changed little from their ancient ancestors, they are the sole surviving members of an ancient group of reptiles, the Rhynchocephalia ("beakheads"). These animals developed before dinosaurs and were once found on every continent except Antarctica. The fossil record shows that all other species of Rhynchocephalia died out 65 million years ago. When New Zealand separated from other land masses, the tuatara survived because of the absence of major predators. Now, however, it is one of the rarest reptiles in the world.

Unlike lizards, tuataras do not have eardrums or a copulatory (reproductive) organ, and there are certain differences in the skeletons. They can produce a croaking sound and are thought to be able to see in the dark. Their eyes are similar in structure to a crocodile's or turtle's. One feature shared with lizards is the "third eye" in the skull. This scale-covered gland is connected to the brain and is sensitive to light, but cannot actually "see." The scientific name *Sphenodon* means "wedge tooth." Unusually, the tuatara's teeth are fused to the jawbone. (In most reptiles teeth can be replaced.)

Home Sweet Habitat

Once common throughout New Zealand, tuataras are now mostly restricted to 32 cool, damp islands off the northeastern coast of North Island and in the Cook Strait area. Tuataras had last been seen on the mainland of New Zealand in the 1860s. Then, in 2008 a tuatara nest was discovered at Karori Sanctuary—the first proven breeding on the mainland for 200 years. The summer temperature on the offshore islands rarely rises above 70°F (21°C) with about 80 percent

---

DATA PANEL

Tuatara (Cook Strait tuatara)

Sphenodon punctatus

Family: Sphenodontidae

World Population: 60,000–100,000

Distribution: Islands off North Island and in the Cook Strait area, New Zealand

Habitat: Cool, damp, rocky islands with soil cover, shrubs, and low vegetation

Size: Length: male up to 24 in (60 cm); female up to 18 in (45 cm). Weight: male up to 2.2 lb (1 kg); female less

Form: Stout-bodied reptile. Spiny crest along back is more prominent in males. Coloration is mainly olive green, sometimes slate gray or pink with overall light speckling. Male usually has a dark patch on each side of the head

Diet: Insects, invertebrates, lizards, chicks and eggs of seabirds, occasionally their own young

Breeding: Females may not breed until they are 11–18 years old; maturity is based on size rather than age. Mating to egg hatching takes 2 years. Eggs laid every 4 years; clutch size 6–15 eggs

Related endangered species: Brother's Island tuatara (*Sphenodon guntheri*) VU

Status: IUCN LC

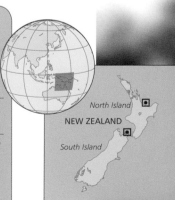

North Island

NEW ZEALAND

South Island

humidity. Unlike other reptiles, tuataras thrive at relatively low temperatures and can still be still active at just above freezing.

The tuatara's habitat has open areas between scrubby growth. The reptiles particularly like a good depth of soil. They dig burrows, but occasionally share those of seabirds. The seabirds are important to the island habitats: their droppings help sustain the vegetation and support the insects on which tuataras feed. On sunny days tuataras bask outside their burrows; the males display by raising their crests and bob their heads to intimidate others. Open areas can become an arena for disputes between males.

Recognizing the unique nature of the tuatara, the New Zealand government made it a strictly protected species in 1895. The Wildlife Act of 1953 enforced complete protection. The tuatara is listed by CITES, which forbids trade in the animals or its products,

Tuatara means spiny (tara) back
(tua) in Maori. The distinctive spiny crest along the reptile's back is less prominent in females.

and access to the islands is strictly controlled. Even so, smuggled specimens have been found in confiscated consignments in the United States.

Enemy Territory
The two main reasons for the tuatara's decline were habitat destruction and predation by rats. Several of New Zealand's reptiles and amphibians are in decline as a result of habitat destruction. Large areas of native vegetation are under cultivation, huge pine forests planted for timber are a prominent feature, and in many parts the vegetation has been destroyed by sheep and goats. Rats have been the tuatara's main enemy. The Polynesian rat arrived with Maori people; brown rats came with European settlers. On some islands where rats have been introduced there are no young tuataras. Rat-eradication programs are part of conservation projects. Another problem is that small islands can only house a limited population of tuataras. There is a proposal to reintroduce tuataras on mainland North Island, but providing a rat-free environment on the mainland would be difficult.

Meanwhile, captive breeding is underway; artificial incubation has shown some success, and hatchlings have been raised to maturity in five years by providing optimal conditions. However, release into the wild is not without its problems.

Pig-nosed Turtle

Carettochelys insculpta

No one knows how many pig-nosed turtles there are in the wild, but its numbers are thought to be declining. Hunting for turtle meat and habitat destruction are the main threats.

The pig-nosed turtle gets its name from its prominent, piglike snout. Its other names—the New Guinea softshell turtle, New Guinea plateless turtle, or the Fly River turtle—come from its first known location: The species was discovered in 1886 in the Strickland River, a tributary of the Fly River in New Guinea. Today its exact distribution is unknown and needs further investigation—it has been recorded in several major rivers around the Fly River. It does not appear to live in estuaries in Australia.

Like sea turtles, the species is totally aquatic, leaving the water only to lay eggs. In keeping with its lifestyle, its limbs are ideally shaped to provide propulsion in water, resembling the flippers of sea turtles. The pig-nosed turtle is omnivorous (feeding on both animal and vegetable substances), although fruit, leaves, and flowers from overhanging riverbank vegetation form the greater part of its diet. The diet varies with the location; in New Guinea mangrove seeds are a main food.

Decline in Numbers

Numbers of pig-nosed turtles in the wild are difficult to estimate, since the reptiles often inhabit remote locations. However, populations have been reported as declining in parts of their range: Australia has put the pig-nosed turtle on the protected species list, and export is banned by law.

The reptile is not protected in New Guinea and is still considered a delicacy by local people in all parts of its range. Controlling the exploitation of the pig-nosed turtle in New Guinea is difficult because of its traditional importance in the diet. In Australia, indigenous people take a small number of the turtles for food, but this is not thought to impact greatly on the population. Otherwise, the species is protected at state and national levels.

Traditional methods of capturing turtles have changed. Formerly they were speared or grabbed in the water. Nowadays fishing lines are more commonly used. In New Guinea motor boats have made rivers more accessible to hunters, leading to bigger catches.

A closed season has been suggested, during which all hunting of pig-nosed turtles would stop. Such a measure could help turtle populations recover from losses sustained through hunting. However, a nonhunting period would be difficult to implement; legal bans on capturing turtles would no doubt be resisted or

DATA PANEL

Pig-nosed turtle

Carettochelys insculpta

Family: Carettochelyidae

World population: Unknown, but about 3,000 in Australia

Distribution: Northern Australia and southern New Guinea (in Papua and Papua New Guinea)

Habitat: Rivers, estuaries (not in Australia), lagoons, and swamps

Size: Length: 22 in (56 cm). Weight: 47 lb (22 kg)

Form: Adults have gray to gray-brown carapace (bony shield); creamy-yellow plastron (lower shell). Carapace is smooth, with raised keel (projection) at rear covered with leathery skin. Hatchlings and juveniles have light radiating marks, a pale streak behind each eye, and white along jaws; shell markings fade with age

Diet: Fruit, leaves, flowers, mollusks, crustaceans, and aquatic insects

Breeding: Clutches of up to 40 eggs laid and buried high in river banks during the dry season

Related endangered species: None

Status: IUCN VU

ignored. The answer may lie in persuasion; the turtles are valuable to the local people, and conservation lies in sustainable harvesting.

Some places where pig-nosed turtles are found have been turned into wildlife sanctuaries, but regulations are often difficult to police. In addition, habitat destruction is not fully controlled outside national parks. Even inside Kakadu National Park in Australia much of the river bank was destroyed by water buffalo wallowing in the mud until a control program was started. The turtle is heavily reliant on riverbanks for both food and nesting sites, so anything that destroys the banks threatens the turtle's existence.

Many human activities have also affected pig-nosed turtle habitat. Mangrove clearance, forestry, and mining—particularly where chemical extraction is used—can destroy river banks. There is also the risk that the rivers will become polluted or choked with silt. In addition, increased demand for water from industry can result in a lowering of the water table, making the turtles' haunts too shallow.

The pig-nosed turtle *has a smooth carapace (bony shield). Unlike in many other turtles, the shield is covered with a leathery skin rather than hard plates.*

Mixed Success with Captive Specimens

It is unusual to find pig-nosed turtles in the United States or British pet trade. The turtle's large size and susceptibility to skin diseases may discourage potential keepers. Unless the water in which the turtles are kept is absolutely clean, captive specimens are at risk from infection. The turtles also have a reputation for being aggressive toward each other in confined quarters. However, a recent report claimed that large numbers are taken for the pet trade for sale in Japan and other countries. The shells command high prices for use in traditional Oriental medicine. Several zoos house collections of the pig-nosed turtle, and a few specimens are in the hands of private collectors. Artificial incubation of eggs has been achieved, suggesting that an adequately funded captive-breeding operation should be possible.

Western Swamp Turtle

Pseudemydura umbrina

The western swamp turtle was first discovered by European settlers in the 19th century, and a scientific description was written in 1901. The turtle then "disappeared" until 1953. Today only a few specimens survive in the wild; investigations have revealed the existence of just two groups in small swamps on the outskirts of Perth in Western Australia.

It is doubtful whether the western swamp turtle ever had a wide distribution, but the specimens surviving now are restricted to a total area of 556 acres (225 ha). Its numbers declined to about 35 until a recovery plan was formulated in 1992. Such scarcity makes it one of the world's rarest reptiles.

The western swamp turtle is the sole surviving member of its genus (group). Fossil records show that it has hardly changed since the early Miocene period, 23 million years ago. Often called the western swamp tortoise, it is one of Australia's smallest chelonian (turtle) species.

Swamp Life

The turtle's habitat has been disrupted by human settlement that reduced the area of the swamp by drainage and land clearance for agriculture, industry, and building. Extraction of water for human use lowered the water table in the region as well. In addition, predation by ravens, foxes, dogs, and cats has taken its toll on young turtles. The two swamps that form its sole habitat in the wild have now been designated as nature reserves. A further 12.4 acres (5 ha) have since been purchased at one of them. The only truly viable wild population is at Ellen Brook Nature Reserve; numbers at Twin Swamps Nature Reserve are maintained by introducing individuals from elsewhere.

The swamps are wet in winter and spring, but dry out in the hot summers. During the wet period the turtles spend much time in the water foraging for food. Their coloring provides effective camouflage against the sand and clay soils of their habitat. As the swamps start to dry out, they bury themselves and estivate (pass the time in a state of torpor), remaining dormant until the rains return. The summer can be a hazardous time, particularly for hatchlings. The young are highly vulnerable to predators and can easily become desiccated (dried out) in hot weather.

AUSTRALIA

Western
Australia

DATA PANEL

**Western swamp turtle
(western swamp tortoise)**

Pseudemydura umbrina

Family: Chelidae

World population: Probably fewer than 50 mature adults in the wild

Distribution: Two small reserves near Perth, Western Australia

Habitat: Swamp with clay and sandy soils, wet in winter, dry in summer

Size: Length: 6 in (15 cm). Weight: male 19.5 oz (555 g); female 14 oz (410 g)

Form: Brown to black shell with yellow patches; head and limbs brown. Feet broad and webbed

Diet: Aquatic insects, small mollusks, crustaceans, tadpoles, and worms

Breeding: Lays 3–5 eggs which hatch in the summer. Each hatchling weighs 0.2–0.24 oz (5–6 g). Mature at 10–15 years of age. Life span up to 50 years

Related endangered species: Mary River turtle *(Elusor macrurus)* EN; Dahl's toad-headed turtle *(Phrynops dahli)* CR; Hoge's sideneck turtle *(P. hogei)* EN

Status: IUCN CR

The western swamp turtle *is still at risk, despite a successful recovery plan that includes habitat regeneration and captive-breeding programs.*

Species Protection

As a result of the rarity of the western swamp turtle the species was listed by CITES in 1975; Australia had already placed a ban on its export some years earlier, and the turtle is also listed under several wildlife-protection plans. However, it takes more than legal protection to save species. The numbers of turtles have to be increased, the habitat improved, and the danger from predators reduced or eliminated. The turtle's low reproductive rate and the 10 to 15 years it takes to reach maturity inevitably hinder its recovery. Given suitable habitat and conditions, however, it can live to about 50 years and ultimately have a long reproductive life.

The swamp turtle rescue operation began in 1988. Led by representatives from various conservation bodies, universities, and Perth Zoo, a recovery plan was formulated. Captive breeding was central to the plan and has continued at Perth Zoo. Groups of turtles in natural enclosures are on view to stimulate public interest. Beginning with only three laying females in 1989, the number of captive-bred animals increased dramatically through the 1990s, although inevitably some eggs are damaged, some do not hatch, and hatchlings occasionally die. However, scores of young turtles have been released into suitably protected swamp reserves.

Habitat improvement has included the construction of fox-proof fences, the control of ravens and other predators, as well as experimental replanting of the habitat. A "corridor" allowing the turtles access between the two sites has also been planted.

Future Prospects

The conservation measures implemented for the western swamp turtle may sound like a success story, but the turtle is still listed as Critically Endangered. Its restricted habitat will only support a certain number of individuals. Part of the recovery plan includes finding more suitable sites. Efforts are also being made to establish a second breeding group in another zoo or establishment in case disease should devastate the group at Perth Zoo or those in the wild. The aim of such precautions is to help ensure that the species will never be lost altogether. Considerable amounts of time, effort, and money have gone into saving the western swamp turtle, but its survival remains precarious in its extremely limited range.

Green and Golden Bell Frog

Litoria aurea

One of Australia's most attractive frogs, the green and golden bell frog has vanished from much of its previous range. The reasons for its decline are not fully understood.

The strikingly colored green and golden bell frog is one of the most extrovert of Australia's frogs. A voracious predator, it will readily eat smaller frogs as well as insects. The frogs tend to be active in and around ponds by day. At night they climb into pondside vegetation in search of prey.

The green and golden bell frog breeds in open, shallow ponds, preferring those with emergent vegetation (plants that have most of their growth above the water, such as bullrushes) around the edges. It chooses short-lived or "ephemeral" ponds that dry out during the winter months. Such ponds are ideal breeding sites because they do not support fish that would prey on the frog's spawn and tadpoles. Breeding takes place in the summer, following rain that fills breeding ponds and floods swamps. The breeding season usually lasts from October to March, but is known to begin as early as August in some places.

During breeding males call from open water, producing a deep, growling sound, described as being like "a distant motorbike changing gear." Females produce a clutch of between 3,000 and 10,000 eggs in a floating, gelatinous mass, which sinks to the bottom of the pond after six to 12 hours. The fertilized eggs hatch after two days, and the larvae grow quite large before metamorphosing (changing their physical form) from tadpoles to frogs about two months later.

Dramatic Decline

An abundant species in the 1950s, the green and golden bell frog's current distribution covers only a small part of its original range. The frogs were previously found at altitudes up to 2,300 feet (700 m), but they are now found only at altitudes below 490 feet (150 m). Consequently, it is confined to a few areas close to the coast of New South Wales, where it is categorized as a Threatened species, and Victoria, where it is Vulnerable.

The reason why the species has declined so dramatically is unknown. Much of its habitat has

DATA PANEL

Green and golden bell frog (green and golden swamp frog)

Litoria aurea

Family: Hylidae

World population: Unknown

Distribution: Coastal areas in southeastern Australia

Habitat: Large and small ponds with marginal vegetation

Size: Length: male 2.2–2.7 in (5.7–6.9 cm); female 2.5–4.2 in (6.5–10.8 cm)

Form: Body flattened and slender. Coloration green above with irregular bronze patches; flanks brown with cream spots; belly white; groin bright turquoise-blue; long legs brown or bronze. Prominent fold of pale skin runs from behind each eye to the groin; irregular white stripe runs from the corner of the mouth to each armpit. Skin is smooth on the back, granular on the belly.

Adhesive disks at the tips of fingers and toes; webbed feet. In the breeding season males develop large nuptial pads on their thumbs

Diet: Invertebrates and other frogs

Breeding: Summer (August–March)

Related endangered species: Several *Litoria* species, notably yellow-spotted tree frog (*Litoria castanea*) CR

Status: IUCN VU

been lost, largely as a result of swamp drainage, but this does not explain why the green and golden bell frog has disappeared so quickly from higher altitudes. It is known that its tadpoles are defenseless against predatory fish. One theory is that the decline is due to the introduction of the North American mosquito fish to control mosquitoes. The evidence is not strong however: There are sites with no mosquito fish where the frogs have also disappeared and others where the fish and frogs coexist. There is also no evidence that the green and golden bell frog has fallen victim to the chytrid fungus that has so seriously affected other frog species farther north, in Queensland.

Population declines were most marked in the 1990s. Of 137 sites where the frogs were reported before this period, they have disappeared from 113. One site that contained an adult population of 138 in 1968 contained only three in 1993. Since 1990 the frog has been reported in only 38 locations, some supporting only five to 15 adult frogs. In New South Wales, the species has disappeared completely from all highland areas above about 820 feet (250 m).

The green and golden bell frog is one of a group of species that has suffered population declines. For example, the yellow-spotted tree frog, which also lived in New South Wales, has not been seen since 1975, although it has been successfully bred in captivity. Captive breeding is also an option for the future conservation of the green and golden bell frog. From a small number of adults a large number of young can be reared for release into the wild. Where the species has been introduced outside Australia—for example, in New Zealand and on some Pacific islands—it has built up large populations.

The green and golden bell frog *gets its name from the coloration on its back: bright green with irregular spots or blotches of gold or bronze.*

Hamilton's Frog

Leiopelma hamiltoni

Precariously confined to a single protected locality, Hamilton's frog is one of the rarest and most primitive frog species in the world.

New Zealand is the natural home of only four species of frog, all belonging to the Leiopelmatidae family. Three fossil species belonging to the same family have been found in New Zealand, suggesting that it was once a diverse and widespread group of frogs. While some frog species introduced from Australia have thrived and spread in New Zealand, the endemic leiopelmatids have vanished from most of the country and are now confined to tiny areas of protected habitat. The rarest of them, Hamilton's frog, is confined to a single rock stack on Stephen's Island, in Cook Strait, where it is found in an area of boulder-strewn ground no more than 656 square yards (600 sq. m) in size.

The leiopelmatids share a number of primitive features with the tailed frog of the Pacific Northwest region of North America. They have nine vertebrae in the backbone (most frogs and toads have eight or fewer) and retain into adulthood the muscles that wag the tail in the tadpole stage. Most remarkably, while most frogs swim by kicking their hindlegs simultaneously, leiopelmatids and the tailed frog kick their legs alternately. This suggests that the two kinds of frog, now living in restricted ranges and separated by thousands of miles of ocean, are the direct descendants of a group of frogs that were the ancestors of all other frogs and toads.

Unusual Breeding Strategy

Hamilton's frog lives in cool, humid habitats in coastal forests. A compact and secretive creature, it is brown in color with dark markings on its flanks. It lacks the tympanum (eardrum) that is visible in most frogs, but has large glands just behind its eyes. Unlike many frogs and toads, it does not require standing water for breeding, instead depositing its eggs on land in damp places under rocks and logs. The eggs are large and contain a lot of water. When they hatch, the larvae remain within the egg capsule and complete their development there, emerging after about 40 days as miniature adults, still with tails. The male remains close to the eggs while they develop; when the froglets emerge, they climb onto his back, where they complete their development.

North Island

Stephens Island

South Island   NEW
ZEALAND

DATA PANEL

Hamilton's frog

Leiopelma hamiltoni

Family: Leiopelmatidae

World population: Fewer than 300

Distribution: Stephens Island, New Zealand

Habitat: Cool, humid areas coastal rock stack

Size: Length: 1.5–2 in (3.5–5 cm)

Form: Light to dark brown with darker markings on the flanks; no tympanum (eardrum); eyes have horizontal pupils

Diet: Small invertebrates

Breeding: Eggs laid on land; larval phase completed in the eggs, which hatch into tiny tailed froglets after about 5 weeks

Related endangered species: Archey's frog (*Leiopelma archeyi*) CR; Maud Island frog (*L. pakeka*) VU; Hochstetter's frog (*L. hochstetteri*) VU

Status: IUCN EN

Driven into Marginal Habitats

Isolated for centuries, New Zealand has become home to a unique endemic fauna (animals found only in one place), none of which are mammals. As a result, when mammals such as rats, cats, goats, and pigs were introduced from other parts of the world, many of the native species, most notably several bird species, were defenseless against the new predators. Several of New Zealand's endemic species are now confined to remote habitats such as high mountain ranges and offshore islands that introduced mammals have not been able to colonize. Probably unable to coexist with introduced rodents, New Zealand's native frogs have retreated to similar remote areas. In addition, much of the damp coastal forest that provides their natural habitat has been destroyed and replaced by farmland.

There are three surviving species of New Zealand frogs in addition to Hamilton's frog. Hochstetter's frog is confined to a few patches of forest on North Island, while Archey's frog occurs only in North Island's Coromandel Mountains. The third surviving species—the Maud Island frog—was thought to be Hamilton's frog until fairly recently, but has been found to be genetically distinct. It is confined to Maud Island in Cook Strait, where it is comparatively common.

Hamilton's frog is threatened by further risks common to many rare species. First, there is the danger that a single environmental catastrophe, such as severe weather or a major pollution event, could wipe out the entire population. Second, there is the problem of inbreeding. In small populations genetic variation is reduced because matings between closely related individuals happen more frequently. Reduced genetic variation limits the capacity of a species to adapt to any changes that may occur in its environment. The conservation action plan instituted for Hamilton's frog includes putting tuatara-proof fencing around the frogs' habitat; moving some frogs to a second island considered to be suitable for the species to thrive on; and regular monitoring of the population.

Hamilton's frog *inhabits a tiny range some 660 square yards (600 sq. m) in size in a cool, humid rock stack on an island in Cook Strait, New Zealand.*

Northern Tinker Frog

Taudactylus rheophilus

Never a common species, the northern tinker frog is one of several frog species that have almost disappeared from high-altitude forest habitat in Queensland's wet tropics. The cause of the declines is not known, but a fungal disease is strongly suspected.

The northern tinker frog was not seen in the wild between 1991 and 1998 and there were fears it had become extinct. Then five individuals were heard calling in a tributary of the Mulgrave River, and there followed sightings from the Mitchell River, Mount Carbine, and Mount Bellenden in Queensland's wet tropical region.

Belonging to the family Myobatrachidae—species that are found in mainland Australia, Tasmania, and New Guinea—it lives in and around some fast-flowing streams at altitudes between 3,080 and 4,590 feet (940 and 1,400 m). Little is known about the natural history of this species. However, it is one of a group of similar frogs in the region that have suffered population declines or disappeared.

A smooth-skinned frog, the northern tinker has no webbing between its fingers or toes. However, it has well-developed adhesive disks at the end of its digits, which enables it to cling to rock faces. It has a rounded snout, and its ears are hidden beneath the skin. It is red-brown or brown with darker markings on the back, its flanks are dark gray or black, and the belly is yellowish. The pale legs are marked with dark bars.

The mating patterns of the northern tinker frog have never been described. It is known that the males call to attract females, producing a soft, metallic call, consisting of a single short note repeated four or five times in quick succession. This "tink-tink" sound gave the species its common name. Its eggs and tadpoles have not been found in nature, although dissected females have been found to contain between 35 and 50 large eggs.

Mysterious Disappearance

It is thought that, like other frogs in the region, the northern tinker declined dramatically in numbers between 1989 and 1991. It is likely that, as in the other species, mortality occurred among adults but not among tadpoles. There is a strong indication that the cause of their decline was the highly virulent chytrid fungus that has affected many frog species, not only in Australia but also in Central America, South America, and Europe.

The chytrid fungus causes a disease called chytridiomycosis. The fungus invades the skin of adult frogs, where it reproduces repeatedly, feeding on keratin—a tough protein found in the skin of most vertebrates. It is not yet known precisely how it kills

DATA PANEL

Northern tinker frog (tinkling frog)

Taudactylus rheophilus

Family: Myobatrachidae

World population: Possibly fewer than 100

Distribution: Northeastern Queensland, Australia

Habitat: Fast-flowing streams in upland rain forest at altitudes between 3,080 and 4,265 ft (940 and 1,300 m)

Size: Length: male 1–1.1 in (2.4–2.7 cm); female 1–1.3 in (2.4–3.1 cm)

Form: Small frog with rounded snout, disks on fingers and toes. Back red-brown or brown with darker markings; flanks dark gray or black; underside yellowish

Diet: Small invertebrates

Breeding: Not observed

Related endangered species: Sharp-snouted day frog (*Taudactylus acutirostris*) CR

Status: IUCN CR

Queensland

AUSTRALIA

frogs. It may be that the fungus interferes with the mechanism of respiration across the skin, causing the frog to suffocate; or the fungus may produce a toxin that poisons its host.

Frog tadpoles do not have keratin in their skin, which is why they are apparently not affected by the fungus. They do, however, have keratin in the horny beak that surrounds their mouth. So while they appear unaffected, when a tadpole metamorphoses into a frog, it is probably already infected by the fungus. As the new adult frogs disperse, they probably carry the fungus with them, spreading it to other populations.

Vulnerability to Extinction

It is typical of the major population declines that have occurred in the last 30 years among amphibians around the world that while some species have declined, others living in the same areas have been unaffected. This suggests that some species of amphibian have some kind of natural vulnerability to whatever process is adversely affecting amphibians.

The northern tinker frog is one of several species that have declined in the wet tropics region of Australia, and all have a number of features in common. They all have very specific habitat requirements and thus a restricted range; they all breed in streams and lay only a small number of eggs. These factors may provide a clue to their population declines. The fact that they breed in streams is consistent with their being attacked by the chytrid fungus, a waterborne pathogen. The northern tinker's low reproductive rate probably also reduces its capacity to recover again following population crashes.

The northern tinker frog *has adhesive disks at the end of its digits that enable it to cling to rock faces as well as slippery leaves.*

Swan Galaxias

Galaxias fontanus

In Australia galaxiids and their relatives fill the niche occupied by salmon and trout elsewhere. It is somewhat ironic, therefore, that the Australian salmonlike fish are under threat of extinction partly because of the unnatural presence of their northern cousins in their waters.

The family Galaxiidae, commonly referred to as galaxias or native minnows, is represented by about 40 species, of which about half occur in Australia. Tasmania is particularly rich in galaxiids, with 15 of the Australian species found there. Some look remarkably like small trout. In fact, one species is so like a trout that it is known as the spotted mountain trout or trout minnow.

Characteristics

Despite overall superficial similarity with their Northern Hemisphere counterparts, galaxiids have a number of features that set them apart. In addition to their small size they have a scaleless body. Perhaps most noticeably, the members of the subfamily Galaxiinae lack an adipose fin—a small, fleshy "second" dorsal (back) fin. The dorsal fin in galaxiids is set so far back on the body that it is more or less in the same spot as the salmon and trout adipose fin. In galaxiids the body is also characteristically "tubular" in cross section—it is rounder than in salmon and trout—while the snout is generally blunt and the head flattened to a greater or lesser extent.

Poorly Known Species

The Swan galaxias, so called because it is known to occur, possibly exclusively, in the upper reaches of the Swan River in eastern Tasmania, is a typical galaxiid.

It is a small species that, like most of the other members of the family, lives its whole life in fresh water. Only a few species, among them the remarkable climbing galaxias, spend any part of their life in the sea, and this only amounts to the first five or six months of their post-hatching development.

The Swan galaxias is believed to have evolved from a landlocked population of ancestral climbing galaxias stock with which it shares the same overall physical characteristics (except size). However, while the biology of climbing galaxias (which can climb waterfalls and rocks) is reasonably well documented, that of the Swan galaxias is very poorly understood.

It is known to feed primarily on aquatic insects, as well as aerial ones that fall into the water, small crustaceans, and algae. It is also known to occur in shoals, rather

DATA PANEL

Swan galaxias

Galaxias fontanus

Family: Galaxiidae

World population: Unknown; once near extinction, but now expanding

Distribution: At most, several headwater streams of the Swan and Macquarie rivers in eastern Tasmania, Australia; several populations from translocated stocks now established

Habitat: Cool, flowing waters; primarily pools and shallow-water stretches of stream edges associated with submerged logs

Size: Length: up to maximum of 5.3 in (13.5 cm)

Form: Tubular body; dorsal (back) and anal (belly) fins set well back; no adipose (second dorsal) fin. Head flattened with large eyes and blunt snout. Brown to olive-colored body with irregular mottling and a light-colored belly. The fins have little color

Diet: Aquatic and terrestrial insects; some aquatic invertebrates and algae

Breeding: No spawning migrations occur. Spawning is restricted to the spring months, but exact spawning sites, or their nature, are unknown

Related endangered species: Barred galaxias (*Galaxias fuscus*) CR; Clarence galaxias (*G. johnstoni*) CR; pedder galaxias (*G. pedderensis*) CR

AUSTRALIA

Tasmania

Swan galaxias
*populations are thought
to be expanding.
However, they are still at
risk from predation by
introduced species.*

than as solitary individuals, and seems to prefer flowing open water, a trait that places it under risk from predators. Some reports, however, say that the species may also be found "along shallow stream margins around log debris."

Spawning was believed to occur during the Australian spring or early summer, this conclusion being based on the presence of small juveniles during January. More recently, however, the consensus is that spawning occurs only in spring, with the post-hatching to juvenile phase lasting about five weeks. During this time the young fish are said to prefer shallow, slow-flowing water. No spawning migration of adults is believed to be undertaken by this species.

Decline and Recovery

At some stage in the past—probably up to the mid- to late 1800s—the Swan galaxias may have occurred throughout the Swan and Macquarie river basins in eastern Tasmania. In 1862, however, the European perch—known in Australia as the redfin perch—was introduced into Tasmania, followed, two years later, by the arrival in Australia of the brown trout.

Together the two predators decimated the local Swan galaxias population, which from the outset presented an easy target because of its tendency (especially seen in juveniles) to gather in open-water pools. The end result of this constant pressure, exerted over more than 100 years, has been a progressive reduction in both total numbers of Swan galaxias, as

well as its range. It is likely that its continued presence in the small, headwater streams of the Swan and Macquarie river tributaries is the direct result of natural barriers such as waterfalls, which prevent the brown trout and redfin perch from gaining access to these water stretches. It is this same "inaccessibility factor" that has been put to work to rescue the species from impending extinction.

In 1989 the Australian Inland Fisheries Commission initiated a relocation program that transferred Swan galaxias stocks from existing populations to suitable alternative locations out of reach of the predators. The results have been encouraging: there are now nine populations based on translocated fish and seven natural populations.

This seems to bode well for the future, but it could be thrown away if any of the predatory exotic species are released into any of the new Swan galaxias strongholds. If this happens, it would undoubtedly spell disaster for the species because next time around it might not prove possible to mount another successful rescue mission.

Trout Cod

Maccullochella macquariensis

The trout cod was once abundant and widespread in the southern part of the Murray-Darling Basin in New South Wales, Australia, as well as in some major rivers of Victoria. Today only two self-sustaining populations are left, one of which became established from stocks introduced in the early 1900s.

As far back as the mid-19th century fishermen knew of the existence of two types of Murray cod. The smaller one—referred to as the blue-nosed cod—was known as a great fighter, struggling to the point of exhaustion whenever it was caught in a net or hook. The larger type was more passive; people also thought that it tasted better.

It was not until 1972 that the true identities of the two cod were finally unraveled. It turned out that the specimen of Murray cod on which the original species description had been based (the holotype) was, in fact, a trout cod and that there were significant differences between it and the larger Murrays. Hence the trout cod, or blue-nosed cod, and the Murray cod now have diferent scientific names.

While not spectacularly colored, the trout cod is a beautiful, impressive animal. It is relatively streamlined and solidly muscled, in keeping with its predatory habits. Its finnage is like the marine groupers and other perchlike fish. The dorsal (back) fin, in particular, has a characteristic spiny front section, followed by a soft, rounded back.

Threats to Survival

The trout cod has been and is still being attacked from several quarters. Overfishing has undoubtedly had a significant effect on populations over the years. Since the trout cod and the Murray cod were long believed to be naturally occurring forms of a single species, angling pressure on the Murray cod has had a carry-over effect on the trout cod. In some areas, such as the Australian Capital Territory, overfishing for Murray cod is thought to have been one of the

---

DATA PANEL

Trout cod

Maccullochella macquariensis

Family: Percichthyidae

World population: Figures unknown, but only 2 self-sustaining populations remain

Distribution: A section of the Murray River and Seven Creeks in Victoria, and the Macquarie River in New South Wales, Australia; hatchery-raised stocks have been introduced to some locations in the region

Habitat: Juveniles shelter under boulders and other cover in fast-flowing stretches of river; adults prefer deep pools

Size: Length: 16–20 in (40–50 cm); up to 32 in (80 cm). Weight: 3.3–6.6 lb (1.5–3 kg); up to 35 lb (16 kg)

Form: Streamlined, powerful body. Blue-gray to brown on top, paler below; overlaid by dark spots and streaks. Fins dusky with white, yellow, or orange edges. Head has deep, gray-black stripe running from tip of snout, through eye, to edge of operculum (gill cover)

Diet: Insects, tadpoles, crustaceans, and fish

Breeding: Pair bonding is believed to exist. Spawning thought to be annual, usually in spring or summer, when water temperatures are 57–73°F (14–23°C). Adhesive eggs laid on logs or rocks; eggs hatch after 5–10 days, depending on temperature. Newly hatched fry are 0.2–0.4 in (0.5–1 cm); they begin feeding some 10 days later. Fully mature at 3–5 years

Related endangered species: Clarence River cod *(Maccullochella ikei)* EN; Mary River cod *(M. peelii mariensis)* CR; Oxleyan pygmy perch *(Nannoperca oxleyana)* EN

Status: IUCN EN

main causes leading to its disappearance from the region's many waterways.

Habitat alteration has also played its part. In the case of the trout cod, the construction of dams and other obstructions has had less of an effect than it might have, since the fish is a nonmigratory species. However, other forms of alteration may have had a more pronounced effect. Former shaded and forested areas have been exposed to the sun. As a result, water temperatures have risen, sediment has increased, and the water quality has deteriorated.

Potentially more dangerous are the effects of introduced species of "exotic" fish, not because of competition for food, but from the new disease organisms (pathogens) that they bring with them. As yet, there is no conclusive evidence that the trout cod is affected, but there is cause for concern. Some other Australian species have been shown to be susceptible to a virus infection (epizootic hematopoietic necrosis) first detected in introduced perch.

The trout cod is distinguished by the spiny dorsal fin on its back. Adult trout cods favor deep pools; juveniles can be found sheltering under boulders in faster stretches of water.

Conservation Measures

No single measure can be considered adequate when it comes to conserving a species like the trout cod. The approach must be multifaceted, ranging from an understanding of the species' biology and ecology to captive breeding for restocking, angling bans, education, and legislation.

All areas are being tackled; hatchery-bred fish are already being used to restock several trout cod habitats. Monitoring will demonstrate over the next few years whether or not released specimens are breeding in the wild. Should it be found that they are, and should the accompanying legislative, ecological, and educational measures be implemented, the future for the trout cod could begin to look a little better.

Categories of Threat

The status categories that appear in the data panel for each species throughout this book are based on those published by the International Union for the Conservation of Nature (IUCN). They provide a useful guide to the current status of the species in the wild, and governments throughout the world use them when assessing conservation priorities and in policy making. However, they do not provide automatic legal protection for the species.

Animals are placed in the appropriate category after scientific research. More species are being added all the time, and animals can be moved from one category to another as their circumstances change.

Extinct (EX)

A group of animals is classified as EX when there is no reasonable doubt that the last individual has died.

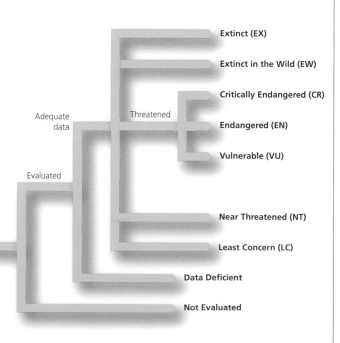

Extinct in the Wild (EW)

Animals in this category are known to survive only in captivity or as a population established artificially by introduction somewhere well outside its former range. A species is categorized as EW when exhaustive surveys throughout the areas where it used to occur consistently fail to record a single individual. It is important that such searches be carried out over all of the available habitat and during a season or time of day when the animals should be present.

Critically Endangered (CR)

The category CR includes animals facing an extremely high risk of extinction in the wild in the immediate future. It includes any of the following:
- Any species with fewer than 50 individuals, even if the population is stable.
- Any species with fewer than 250 individuals if the population is declining, badly fragmented, or all in one vulnerable group.
- Animals from larger populations that have declined by 80 percent within 10 years (or are predicted to do so) or three generations, whichever is the longer.

The IUCN categories *of threat (left). The system displayed has operated for new and reviewed assessments since January 2001.*

• Species living in a very small area—defined as under 39 square miles (100 sq. km).

Endangered (EN)

A species is EN when it is not CR but is nevertheless facing a very high risk of extinction in the wild in the near future. It includes any of the following:

• A species with fewer than 250 individuals remaining, even if the population is stable.

• Any species with fewer than 2,500 individuals if the population is declining, badly fragmented, or all in one vulnerable subpopulation.

• A species whose population is known or expected to decline by 50 percent within 10 years or three generations, whichever is the longer.

• A species whose range is under 1,900 square miles (5,000 sq. km), and whose range, numbers, or population levels are declining, fragmented, or fluctuating wildly.

• Species for which there is a more than 20 percent likelihood of extinction in the next 20 years or five generations, whichever is the longer.

Vulnerable (VU)

A species is VU when it is not CR or EN but is facing a high risk of extinction in the wild in the medium-term future. It includes any of the following:

• A species with fewer than 1,000 mature individuals remaining, even if the population is stable.

• Any species with fewer than 10,000 individuals if the population is declining, badly fragmented, or all in one vulnerable subpopulation.

Fewer than 1,000 *numbats (left) remain in the wild. These beautifully marked marsupials live in a small area of Western Australia.*

AUSTRALIA

Western Australia

• A species whose population is known, believed, or expected to decline by 20 percent within 10 years or three generations, whichever is the longer.
• A species whose range is less than 772 square miles (20,000 sq. km), and whose range, numbers, or population structure are declining, fragmented, or fluctuating wildly.
• Species for which there is a more than 10 percent likelihood of extinction in the next 100 years.

Near Threatened/Least Concern (since 2001)

In January 2001 the classification of lower-risk species was changed. Near Threatened (NT) and Least Concern (LC) were introduced as separate categories. They replaced the previous Lower Risk (LR) category with its subdivisions of Conservation Dependent (LRcd), Near Threatened (LRnt), and Least Concern (LRlc). From January 2001 all new assessments and reassessments must adopt NT or LC if relevant. But the older categories still apply to some animals until they are reassessed, and will also be found in this book.
• Near Threatened (NT)
Animals that do not qualify for CR, EN, or VU categories now but are close to qualifying or are likely to qualify for a threatened category in the future.
• Least Concern (LC)
Animals that have been evaluated and do not qualify for CR, EN, VU, or NT categories.

Lower Risk (before 2001)

• Conservation Dependent (LRcd)
Animals whose survival depends on an existing conservation program
• Near Threatened (LRnt)
Animals for which there is no conservation program but that are close to qualifying for VU category.
• Least Concern (LRlc)
Species that are not conservation dependent or near threatened.

The green and gold *bell frog of Australia's Victoria and New South Wales states is known to have declined, although the reasons for this fall in numbers is not fully understood. Its status is now described as Vulnerable.*

Data Deficient (DD)

A species or population is DD when there is not enough information on abundance and distribution to assess the risk of extinction. In some cases, when the species is thought to live only in a small area, or a considerable period of time has passed since the species was last recorded, it may be placed in a threatened category as a precaution.

Not Evaluated (NE)

Such animals have not yet been assessed.

Note: a colored panel in each entry in this book indicates the current level of threat to the species. The two new categories (NT and LC) include the earlier Lower Risk categories (LRcd and LRnt); the old LRlc is included along with Data Deficient (DD) and Not Evaluated (NE) under "Other," abbreviated to "O."

CITES *lists animals in the major groups in three appendices, depending on the level of threat posed by international trade.*

	Appendix I	Appendix II	Appendix III
Mammals	297 species 23 subspecies 2 populations	492 species 5 subspecies 5 populations	44 species 10 subspecies
Birds	156 species 11 subspecies 2 populations	1,275 species 2 subspecies	24 species
Reptiles	76 species 5 subspecies 1 population	582 species 6 populations	56 species
Amphibians	17 species	113 species	1 species
Fish	15 species	81 species	
Invertebrates	64 species 5 subspecies	2,142 species 1 subspecies	17 species 3 subspecies

CITES APPENDICES

Appendix I lists the most endangered of traded species, namely those that are threatened with extinction and will be harmed by continued trade. These species are usually protected in their native countries and can only be imported or exported with a special permit. Permits are required to cover the whole transaction—both exporter and importer must prove that there is a compelling scientific justification for moving the animal from one country to another. This includes transferring animals between zoos for breeding purposes. Permits are only issued when it can be proved that the animal was legally acquired and that the remaining population will not be harmed by the loss.

Appendix II includes species not currently threatened with extinction but could easily become so if trade is not carefully controlled. Some common animals are listed here if they resemble endangered species so closely that criminals could try to sell the rare species pretending they were a similar common one. Permits are required to export such animals, with requirements similar to those Appendix I species.

Appendix III species are those that are at risk or protected in at least one country. Other nations may be allowed to trade in animals or products, but they may need to prove that they come from safe populations.

CITES designations are not always the same for every country. In some cases individual countries can apply for special permission to trade in a listed species. For example, they might have a safe population of an animal that is very rare elsewhere. Some African countries periodically apply for permission to export large quantities of elephant tusks that have been in storage for years, or that are the product of a legal cull of elephants. This is controversial because it creates an opportunity for criminals to dispose of black market ivory by passing it off as coming from one of those countries where elephant products are allowed to be exported. If you look up the African elephant, you will see that it is listed as CITES I, II, and III, depending on the country location of the different populations.

Organizations

The human race is undoubtedly nature's worst enemy, but we can also help limit the damage caused by the rapid increase in our numbers and activities. There have always been people eager to protect the world's beautiful places and to preserve its most special animals, but it is only quite recently that the conservation message has begun to have a real effect on everyday life, government policy, industry, and agriculture.

Early conservationists were concerned with preserving nature for the benefit of people. They acted with an instinctive sense of what was good for nature and people, arguing for the preservation of wilderness and animals in the same way as others argued for the conservation of historic buildings or gardens. The study of ecology and environmental science did not really take off until the mid-20th century, and it took a long time for the true scale of our effect in the natural world to become apparent. Today the conservation of wildlife is based on far greater scientific understanding, but the situation has become much more complex and urgent in the face of human development.

By the mid-20th century extinction was becoming an immediate threat. Animals such as the passenger pigeon, quagga, and thylacine had disappeared despite last-minute attempts to save them. More and more species were discovered to be at risk, and species-focused conservation groups began to appear. In the early days there was little that any of these organizations could do but campaign against direct killing. Later they became a kind of conservation emergency service—rushing to the aid of seriously threatened animals in an attempt to save the species. But as time went on, broader environmental issues began to receive the urgent attention they needed. Research showed time and time again that saving species almost always comes down to addressing the problem of habitat loss. The world is short of space, and ensuring that there is enough for all the species is very difficult.

Conservation is not just about animals and plants, nor even the protection of whole ecological systems. Conservation issues are so broad that they touch almost every aspect of our lives, and successful measures often depend on the expertise of biologists, ecologists, economists, diplomats, lawyers, social scientists, and businesspeople. Conservation is all about cooperation and teamwork. Often it is also about helping people benefit from taking care of their wildlife. The organizations involved vary from small groups of a few dozen enthusiasts in local communities to vast, multinational operations.

The IUCN

With so much activity based in different countries, it is important to have a worldwide overview, some way of coordinating what goes on in different parts of the planet. That is the role of the International Union for the Conservation of Nature (IUCN), also referred to as the World Conservation Union. It began life as the International Union for the Preservation of Nature in 1948, becoming the IUCN in 1956. It is relatively new compared to the Sierra Club, Flora and Fauna International, and the Royal Society for the Protection of Birds. It was remarkable in that its founder members included governments, government agencies, and nongovernmental organizations. In the years following the appalling destruction of World War II, the IUCN was born out of a desire to act together to safeguard the future.

The mission of the IUCN is to influence, encourage, and assist societies throughout the world to conserve the diversity of nature and natural systems. It seeks to ensure that the use of natural resources is fair and

Twin Falls *in Kakadu National Park. The park is Australia's largest protected land area and receives the protection afforded by World Heritage status. It lies in the Northern Territory.*

ecologically sustainable. Based in Switzerland, the IUCN has over 1,000 permanent staff and the help of 11,000 volunteer experts from about 180 countries. The work of the IUCN is split into six commissions, which deal with protected areas, policy-making, ecosystem management, education, environmental law, and species survival. The Species Survival Commission (SSC) has almost 7,000 members, all experts in the study of plants and animals. Within the SSC there are Specialist Groups concerned with the conservation of different types of animals, from cats to flamingos, deer, ducks, bats, and crocodiles. Some particularly well-studied animals, such as the African elephant and the polar bear, have their own specialist groups.

Perhaps the best-known role of the IUCN SSC is in the production of the Red Data Books, or Red Lists. First published in 1966, the books were designed to be easily updated, with details of each species on a different page that could be removed and replaced as new information came to light.

By 2013 the Red Lists include information on about 53,000 types of animal, of which more than 11,000 are threatened with extinction. Gathering this amount of information together is a huge task, but it provides an invaluable conservation resource. The Red Lists are continually updated and are now available on the Internet. The Red Lists are the basis for the categories of threat used in this book.

IUCN

CITES is the Convention on International Trade in Endangered Species of Wild Fauna and Flora (also known as the Washington Convention). Currently 175 nations have agreed to implement the CITES regulations. Exceptions to the convention include Iraq and North Korea, which, for the time being at least, have few trading links with the rest of the world. Trading in animals and their body parts has been a major factor in the decline of some of the world's rarest species. The IUCN categories draw attention to the status of rare species, but they do not confer any legal protection. That is done through national laws.

Conventions serve as international laws. In the case of CITES, lists (called appendices) are agreed on internationally and reviewed every few years. The appendices list the species that are threatened by international trade. Animals are assigned to Appendix I when all trade is forbidden. Any specimens of these species, alive or dead (or skins, feathers, etc.), will be confiscated by customs at international borders, seaports, or airports. Appendix II species can be traded internationally, but only under strict controls. Wildlife trade is often valuable in the rural economy, and this raises difficult questions about the relative importance of animals and people. Nevertheless, traders who ignore CITES rules risk heavy fines or imprisonment. Some rare species—even those with the highest IUCN categories (many bats and frogs, for example)—may have no CITES protection simply because they have no commercial value. Trade is then not really a threat.

WILDLIFE CONSERVATION ORGANIZATIONS

BirdLife International
BirdLife International is a partnership of 60 organizations working in more than 100 countries. Most partners are national nongovernmental conservation groups. Others include large bird charities. By working within BirdLife International, even small organizations can be effective globally as well as on a local scale.
www.birdlife.org

Conservation International (CI)
Founded in 1987, Conservation International works closely with the IUCN and has a similar multinational approach.
www.conservation.org

Durrell Wildlife Conservation Trust (DWCT)
The Durrell Wildlife Conservation Trust was founded by the British naturalist and author Gerald Durrell in 1963. The trust is based at Durrell's zoo on Jersey in the Channel Islands. Jersey Zoo and the DWCT were instrumental in saving many species from extinction, including the pink pigeon, Mauritius kestrel, Waldrapp ibis, St. Lucia parrot, and Telfair's skink.
www.durrell.org

Fauna & Flora International (FFI)
Founded in 1903, this organization has had various name changes. It began life as a society for protecting large mammals, but has broadened its scope. It was involved in saving the Arabian oryx from extinction.
www.fauna-flora.org

National Audubon Society
John James Audubon was an American naturalist and wildlife artist who died in 1851, 35 years before the society that bears his name was founded. The first Audubon Society was established by George Bird Grinnell in protest against the appalling overkill of birds for meat, feathers, and sport. By the end of the 19th century there were Audubon Societies in 15 states, and they later became part of the National Audubon Society, which funds scientific research programs, publishes magazines and journals, manages wildlife sanctuaries, and advises state and federal governments on conservation.
www.audubon.org

The Sierra Club
The Sierra Club was started in 1892 by John Muir. It was through Muir's efforts that the first national parks, including Yosemite, Sequoia, and Mount Rainier, were established. Today the Sierra Club remains dedicated to the preservation of wild places for the benefit of wildlife and people.
www.sierraclub.org

World Wide Fund for Nature (WWF)
The World Wide Fund for Nature, formerly the World Wildlife Fund, was born in 1961. It was a joint venture between the IUCN, several existing conservation organizations, and a number of successful businesspeople. WWF was big, well-funded, and high profile from the beginning. Its familiar giant panda emblem is instantly recognizable.
www.wwf.org

More Endangered Animals

This is the second series of Facts at Your Fingertips: Endangered Animals. Many other endangered animals were included in the first series, which was broken down by animal class, as follows:

BIRDS

Northern Brown Kiwi
Galápagos Penguin
Bermuda Petrel
Andean Flamingo
Northern Bald Ibis
White-headed Duck
Nene
Philippine Eagle
Spanish Imperial Eagle
Red Kite
California Condor
Mauritius Kestrel
Whooping Crane
Takahe
Kakapo
Hyacinth Macaw
Pink Pigeon
Spotted Owl
Bee Hummingbird
Regent Honeyeater
Blue Bird of Paradise
Raso Lark
Gouldian Finch

FISH

Coelacanth
Great White Shark
Common Sturgeon
Danube Salmon
Lake Victoria Haplochromine Cichlids
Dragon Fish
Silver Shark
Whale Shark
Northern Bluefin Tuna
Masked Angelfish
Big Scale Archerfish
Bandula Barb
Mekong Giant Catfish
Alabama Cavefish
Blind Cave Characin
Atlantic Cod
Mountain Blackside Dace
Lesser Spiny Eel
Australian Lungfish
Paddlefish
Ornate Paradisefish
Knysna Seahorse
Spring Pygmy Sunfish

INVERTEBRATES

Broad Sea Fan
Giant Gippsland Earthworm
Edible Sea-Urchin
Velvet Worms
Southern Damselfly
Orange-spotted Emerald
Red-kneed Tarantula
Kauai Cave Wolf Spider
Great Raft Spider
European Red Wood Ant
Hermit Beetle
Blue Ground Beetle
Birdwing Butterfly
Apollo Butterfly
Avalon Hairstreak Butterfly
Hermes Copper Butterfly
Giant Clam
California Bay Pea Crab
Horseshoe Crab
Cushion Star
Freshwater Mussel
Starlet Sea Anemone
Partula Snails

MAMMALS OF THE NORTHERN HEMISPHERE

Asiatic Lion
Tiger
Clouded Leopard
Iberian Lynx
Florida Panther
Wildcat
Gray Wolf
Swift Fox
Polar Bear
Giant Panda
European Mink
Pine Marten
Black-footed Ferret
Wolverine
Sea Otter
Steller's Sea Lion
Mediterranean Monk Seal
Florida Manatee
Przewalski's Wild Horse
American Bison
Arabian Oryx
Wild Yak
Ryukyu Flying Fox

MAMMALS OF THE SOUTHERN HEMISPHERE

Cheetah
Leopard
Jaguar
Spectacled Bear
Giant Otter
Amazon River Dolphin
Sperm Whale
Blue Whale
Humpback Whale
Proboscis Monkey
Chimpanzee
Mountain Gorilla
Orang-Utan
Ruffed Lemur
African Elephant
Black Rhinoceros
Giant Otter Shrew
Mulgara
Kangaroo Island Dunnart
Marsupial Mole
Koala
Long-beaked Echidna
Platypus

REPTILES AND AMPHIBIANS

Blunt-nosed Leopard Lizard
Pygmy Blue-tongued Skink
Komodo Dragon
Hawksbill Turtle
Yellow-blotched Sawback Map Turtle
Galápagos Giant Tortoise
Jamaican Boa
Woma Python
Milos Viper
Chinese Alligator
American Crocodile
Gharial
Gila Monster
Japanese Giant Salamander
Olm
Mallorcan Midwife Toad
Golden Toad
Western Toad
Golden Mantella
Tomato Frog
Gastric-brooding Frog

GLOSSARY

adaptation Features of an animal that adjust it to its environment; may be produced by evolution—e.g., camouflage coloration

adaptive radiation Where a group of closely related animals (e.g., members of a family) have evolved differences from each other so that they can survive in different niches

amphibian Any cold-blooded vertebrate of the class Amphibia, typically living on land but breeding in the water; e.g., frogs, toads, newts, and salamanders

anterior The front part of an animal

arboreal Living in trees

bill The jaws of a bird, consisting of two bony mandibles, upper and lower, and their horny sheaths

biodiversity The variety of species and the variation within them

biome A major world landscape characterized by having similar plants and animals living in it, e.g., desert, rain forest, forest

breeding season The entire cycle of reproductive activity, from courtship, pair formation (and often establishment of territory) through nesting to independence of young

brood The young hatching from a single clutch of eggs

canine tooth A sharp stabbing tooth usually longer than the rest

carapace The upper part of a shell in a chelonian

carnivore An animal that eats other animals

carrion Rotting flesh of dead animals

chelonian A turtle or tortoise

cloaca Cavity in the pelvic region into which the alimentary canal, genital, and urinary ducts open

diurnal Active during the day

DNA (deoxyribonucleic acid) The substance that makes up the main part of the chromosomes of all living things; contains the genetic code that is handed down from generation to generation

dormancy A state in which—as a result of hormone action—growth is suspended and metabolic activity is reduced to a minimum

dorsal Relating to the back or spinal part of the body; usually the upper surface

ecology The study of plants and animals in relation to one another and to their surroundings

ecosystem A whole system in which plants, animals, and their environment interact

ectotherm Animal that relies on external heat sources to raise body temperature; also known as "cold-blooded"

endemic Found only in one geographical area, nowhere else

eutrophication An increase in the nutrient chemicals (nitrate, phosphate, etc.) in water, sometimes occurring naturally and sometimes caused by human activities, e.g., by the release of sewage or agricultural fertilizers

extinction Process of dying out at the end of which the very last individual dies, and the species is lost forever

feral Domestic animals that have gone wild and live independently of people

gene The basic unit of heredity, enabling one generation to pass on characteristics to its offspring

gestation The period of pregnancy in mammals, between fertilization of the egg and birth of the baby

herbivore An animal that eats plants (grazers and browsers are herbivores)

hibernation Becoming inactive in winter, with lowered body temperature to save energy. Hibernation takes place in a special nest or den called a hibernaculum

homeotherm An animal that can maintain a high and constant body temperature by means of internal processes; also called "warm-blooded"

inbreeding Breeding among closely related animals (e.g., cousins), leading to weakened genetic composition and reduced survival rates

incubation The act of keeping eggs warm for the period from laying the eggs to hatching

insectivore Animal that feeds on insects. Also used as a group name for hedgehogs, shrews, moles, etc.

joey A young kangaroo living in its mother's pouch

keratin Tough, fibrous material that forms hair, feathers, nails, and protective plates on the skin of vertebrate animals

larva An immature form of an animal that develops into an adult form through metamorphosis

mammal Any animal of the class Mammalia—a warm-blooded vertebrate having mammary glands in the female that produce milk with which it nurses its young. The class includes bats, primates, rodents, and whales

marsupial Mammals that give birth to incompletely developed young that are carried and suckled in a pouch on the mother's belly. Kangaroos are marsupials.

metabolic rate The rate at which chemical activities occur within animals, including the exchange of gasses in respiration and the liberation of energy from food

metamorphosis The transformation of a larva into an adult

omnivore An animal that eats a wide range of both animal and vegetable food

parasite An animal or plant that lives on or within the body of another (the host) from which it obtains nourishment. The host is often harmed by the association

pheromone Scent produced by animals to enable others to find and recognize them

placenta The structure that links an embryo to its mother during pregnancy, allowing exchange of chemicals between them

posterior The hind end or behind another structure

quadruped Any animal that walks on four legs

raptor Bird with hooked bill and strong feet with sharp claws (talons) for seizing, killing, and dealing with prey; also known as birds of prey

reptile Any member of the class of cold-blooded vertebrates, Reptilia, including crocodiles, lizards, snakes, tortoises, turtles, and tuataras. Reptiles are characterized by an external covering of scales or horny plates. Most are egg-layers, but some give birth to live young

spawning The laying and fertilizing of eggs by fish and amphibians

vertebrate Animal with a backbone (e.g., fish, mammal, reptile), usually with skeleton made of bones, but sometimes softer cartilage

FURTHER RESEARCH

Books

Mammals

Cronin, L., *Cronin's Guide to Australian Wildlife*, Allen & Unwin, Sydney, Australia, 2007

Flannery, T., *Mammals of New Guinea*, The Australian Museum, Sydney, Australia, 1990

Fuentes, Mariana, *Dhyum the Dugong*, Reef and Rainforest Research Centre, Cairns, Australia, 2012

Macdonald, David, ed, *The New Encyclopedia of Mammals,* Oxford University Press, Oxford, U.K., 2009

Menkhorst, P., and F. Knight. *A Field Guide to Australian Mammals*, Oxford University Press, Melbourne, Australia, 2004.

Richardson, Ken, *Australia's Amazing Kangaroos*, CSIRO Publishing, Collingwood, Australia, 2012

Wilson, Don E., Mittermeier, Russell A., *Handbook of Mammals of the World Vol 1,* Lynx Edicions, Barcelona, Spain, 2009

Birds

Attenborough, David, *The Life of Birds,* BBC Books, London, U.K., 1998

Beehler, B.M., *Birds of New Guinea*, Princeton University Press, U.S., 2013

BirdLife International, *State of the World's Birds: Indicators for our Changing World*, BirdLife International, Cambridge, U.K., 2008

del Hoyo, J., Elliott, A., and Sargatal, J., eds, *Handbook of Birds of the World Vols 1 to 15,* Lynx Edicions, Barcelona, Spain, 1992–2013

Harris, Tim, *Migration Hotspots of the World*, Bloomsbury/RSPB, London, U.K., 2013

Rowland, Peter, *Bowerbirds*, CSIRO Publishing, Collingwood, Australia, 2008

Stattersfield, A., Crosby, M., Long, A., and Wege, D., eds, *Endemic Bird Areas of the World: Priorities for Biodiversity Conservation,* BirdLife International, Cambridge, U.K., 1998

Fish

Buttfield, Helen, *The Secret Lives of Fishes*, Abrams, U.S., 2000

Dawes, John, and Campbell, Andrew, eds, *The New Encyclopedia of Aquatic Life, Facts On File*, New York, U.S., 2004

Reptiles and Amphibians

Anstis, Marion, *Tadpoles and Frogs of Australia*, New Holland, Sydney, Australia, 2013.

Hofrichter, Robert, *Amphibians: The World of Frogs, Toads, Salamanders, and Newts*, Firefly Books, Canada, 2000

Lutz, Richard, *Tuatara: A Living Fossil*, Dimi Press, Salem, OR, U.S., 2006

Taylor, Barbara, and O'Shea, Mark, *Great Big Book of Snakes and Reptiles*, Hermes House, London, U.K., 2006

Tyler, Michael, and Frank Knight, *Field Guide to the Frogs of Australia*, CSIRO Publishing, Collingwood, Australia, 2011

General

Allaby, Michael, *A Dictionary of Ecology*, Oxford University Press, New York, U.S., 2010

Douglas, Dougal, and others, *Atlas of Life on Earth*, Barnes & Noble, New York, U.S., 2001

Web sites

www.nature.nps.gov/ United States National Park Service wildlife site

www.abcbirds.org/ American Bird Conservancy. Articles, information about bird conservation in the Americas

www.birlife.org/ The site of BirdLife International, highlighting projects to protect the populations of endangered species

www.cites.org/ CITES and IUCN listings. Search for animals by order, family, genus, species, or common name. Location by country and explanation of reasons for listings

www.cmc-ocean.org Facts, figures, and quizzes about marine life

www.darwinfoundation.org/ Charles Darwin Research Center

www.edgeofexistence.com Highlights and conserves one-of-a-kind species that are on the verge of extinction

www.endangeredspecie.com
Information, links, books, and publications about rare and endangered species. Also includes information about conservation efforts and organizations

www.fauna-flora.org Information about animals and plants around the world on the site of the Flora and Fauna Conservation Society

www.forests.org/ Includes forest conservation answers to queries

www.iucn.org/ Details of species, IUCN listings, and IUCN publications. Link to online Red Lists of threatened species at: www.iucnredlist.org

www.panda.org/ World Wide Fund for Nature (WWF). Newsroom, press releases, government reports, campaigns. Themed photogallery

www.wcs.org/ Wildlife Conservation Society site. Information on projects to help endangered animals in every continent.

www.wdcs.org/ Whale and Dolphin Conservation Society site. News, projects, and campaigns. Sightings database

INDEX